THE CLOVERDALE FORAGER

THE CLOVERDALE FORAGER

YOUR GUIDEBOOK FOR GATHERING, PREPARING, AND SAVORING WILD FOOD

JIM DeMARTINI

Illustrations by Sophia DeMartini

The Cloverdale Forager

Your Guidebook for Gathering, Preparing, and Savoring Wild Food

Jim DeMartini

Published by Jim DeMartini

ISBN: 979-8-218-09080-7

For the love of being outside . . .

PREFACE

The stories set out in this book were originally published between 2007 and 2012 in the *Cloverdale Reveille* as the series "The Cloverdale Forager."

Back then, I'd been practicing law in Cloverdale for thirty years and had represented the paper through several owners and publishers. The series was started during the reign of Bonnie Jean Hanchett whose family owned and published the paper as the oldest continuously published weekly in California. Alas, like many of the great papers, the *Reveille* has been overcome by the digital tsunami.

BJ was a pioneer newswoman. She became a close friend and confidant to me over the years she ran the paper. Her family, son Val and daughter-in-law Neena, ran the composition and advertising ends of the paper with BJ at the editorial helm. Together, they encouraged me to tell my story to the *Reveille's* readers.

Writing the articles was a creative break from the everyday grind of lawyering. For all the good I figured I was providing society with my dedication to truth, justice, and the American way, nobody in Cloverdale had much to say about my dedication to the law, but everybody wanted to talk about the latest *Forager* article recipe.

I owe any skill I might bring to outdoor writing to my two outdoor writing heroes, the late Jim Freeman, and Tom Stienstra of the *San Francisco Chronicle*. My interest in writing the articles was nurtured by my reading of Peter Howorth's *Foraging Along the California Coast* (Capra Press, 1977). I'll admit stealing much of my inspiration from Peter's book and I commend it to your attention.

Thanks also to my daughter, Sophia DeMartini, for her skillful pencil renditions of the game that has graced my bag and table.

CONTENTS

ABALONE

A nybody who tells you that they love abalone for its fabulous taste is not someone who gathers their own abalone. It's not that abalone doesn't taste good–it does indeed, given the right preparation and/or consumption setting (see below).

I firmly believe that given a choice, most people would, after they'd tasted both, opt for a nicely barbequed, medium-rare piece of fresh albacore filet over a breaded and fried slice of abalone. To those who gather the overgrown snail, abalone is loved less for reasons epicurean than for reasons found only off the beach.

"Abalone-love" is a dead flat April morning fifty yards off the beach. The fog is still hanging low and the sun has yet to show itself over the redwoods. It's the glimmering iridescence of kelp slowly waving in a gentle surge of Pacific water through which you can see twenty feet or more.

It's the unmistakable sweet/tart smell that abalone, and other reef dwellers, give off at low tide that makes the air smell like the very essence of marine life. It's lying silently, with your facemask half in and half out of the water–a harbor seal, looking for a free meal above and a greenling protecting its crevasse below.

You just can't get the sense of tranquility, and inclusion in nature, anywhere else, short of your mother's womb.

And then you see them–blithely sticking to rocks at the bottom or wedged into cracks that twist and widen like miniature mountain valleys. On a good day, you can pick the big ones out from the smaller "clickers," so named because, at slightly more than the seven-inch minimum size, they barely touch each point of a metal abalone gage.

Dropping down to the seafloor to get an ab can be as pleasant as slipping to the bottom of a swimming pool or as complicated as groping through a washing machine, in the dark, while holding your breath in forty-seven-degree water. (The second example is not why I love abalone.)

Prying an abalone off a rock is a relatively simple function, unless it happens to have sensed you coming and chooses to clamp itself tight to a rock, or you happen to start running out of air. In either event, freeing the ab from its resting place becomes problematic.

The best abalone irons, one of which you must have in your possession, along with a gauge, are made from automobile leaf springs. The one I own was given to me by my father sixty years ago and has taken hundreds of abalone.

The rules for tagging your abalone and recording your take on a report card are simple, but you have to pay attention to the rules. The Department of Fish and Game wardens on the coast are strictly enforcing the rules. If you do it wrong it can cost you a couple of thousand dollars in fines, as well as confiscation of both your abalone and your dive equipment, and, if you aggravate the warden, your vehicle. The rules are there for a good reason. The resource is delicate and needs constant vigilance.

COOKING ABALONE

In fact, I do not disparage the breading of, and subsequent frying of, abalone steaks. I grew up on them and still cook them that way most of the time. It took the Old Italians years to convince me to slice an abalone top to bottom, across the grain, rather than what I was taught (by other Old Italians): horizontally.

Differing techniques also abound when it comes to how to pound an abalone. Pounding abalone is basically an absolute requirement to render them edible, although if you bake a whole ab for about three hours, it will eventually become tender. The most effective technique is the way Doug Dilley taught me. First, you cut the leg of an old pair of jeans and tie one end closed. Then you put a cleaned abalone in the denim tube and beat the entire beast with a bat. This relaxes the whole ab and the steaks require far less individual pounding.

I don't do it much anymore, but if you sort through the guts long enough, you will find abalone pearls! Apparently, abalones create pearls in the same manner as oysters, covering an irritating grain of sand in pearlescence.

Healdsburg vet Ben Baldwin's method of cooking abalone chowder demonstrates the secret of cooking abalone. Either cook it forever, or hardly at all. Ben takes the hard trimmings from the outside of the abalone's foot, scrubs the black off, grinds them in a meat grinder, and boils them for three hours. The result is perfect abalone broth and very tender meat. You build your standard chowder around the broth and meat, adding milk or cream, potatoes, onions, and celery, and whatever else you like in your chowder. Thinly slice and pound the rest of the abalone as though you were making streaks, chop the slices into chowder size pieces, and add to the chowder for the last minute of cooking. Unbelievable.

The absolute best tasting abalone, however, is eaten at the beach. When I was in college, we'd leave Berkeley at 2:00 a.m. with a fifty-gallon oil drum lid that we'd sanded clean and hammered into a shallow wok. While still in our wet suits, we'd pound abalone steaks with our cutting boards balanced on wash rocks. Throw a cube of butter in the lid while it was suspended over a drift wood fire, and fry steaks that were fifteen minutes out of the ocean. Until you've tried it, you can't discern the unbelievably different taste between an abalone that is fresh from the water on one that has been out of the water for an hour or two. Indescribable. Worthy of love.

Note: This article was written before the California Department of Fish and Wildlife closed the sport harvest of abalone throughout California. The reasons for the closure are lengthy but climate change appears to be the primary cause. The abalone population started a precipitous decline when ocean temperatures began to rise quickly in the 1990s. This temperature increase brought with it a "wasting disease" that killed off the indigenous sunflower sea stars-starfish to most of us. Once the sea stars began to die off the population of a particularly aggressive small light-blue sea urchin, the sea star's favorite food, exploded. The urchins immediately took over the rocky reefs off the Sonoma coast devouring every scrap of bull kelp they could find. It was unbelievably frightening to see how once verdant kept forests became underwater deserts virtually overnight. The loss of kelp, the abalones' primary food, starved the abalone nearly to extinction. The state closed the take of abalone to try to preserve the species. There are no plans to reopen the harvest.

ACORNS

T he looks on the other lawyers' faces said it all: "He's gone over the edge!"

Their concern was understandable. Just minutes after leaving a deposition at a friend's office, I was on my hands and knees, on his lawn, scooping up oblong nuggets of sustenance that had fallen from a tan bark oak in his front yard. This is the first law of gathering acorns: get them when you can.

The second law is patience . . . lots of patience.

To the native Pomo, the acorn was the basic provider of life. They ate acorns nearly every day of their lives. The wild game on which the tribe subsisted, lived on acorns much of the year.

There are nearly a dozen different oaks that are indigenous to the country between Cloverdale and the coast. Each produces an acorn sometime during the year.

I've discovered that there is still a dispute between the senior women of the Pomo tribe as to where the best acorns come from. Some say the dry hills to the east, with the tan-bark and valley oaks, grow the best acorns. Some say the wetter hills toward the coast with the live oaks and black oaks are better suited to producing acorns.

Acorns are a remarkably balanced food source. The nut meat of the acorn is 31.4 percent water, 3.44 percent protein, 13.55 percent fats, 8.60 percent fiber, and 41.81 percent carbohydrates. Acorns that have already sprouted have a higher sugar, and lower starch, content than do newly dropped acorns.

The Pomos gathered acorns almost all year, but the primary harvest was in the fall when the nuts fell. This is when the first law of acorns comes into play. Almost everything in the forest around here eats acorns. Deer eat them, squirrels eat them, tree rats eat them, crows eat them, (these days turkeys and pigs eat them, but the Pomo didn't have turkeys or pigs) grouse eat them, raccoons eat them, and bears eat them. Pretty much anything that can swallow an acorn eats them. When they hit the ground, the first omnivore there gets the acorn. Get them when you can.

The second law, patience, arises in the preparation of acorns for consumption.

Having dealt with the acorn preparation issue, my respect for the patience of the people who lived on acorns is immense.

Once you gather them, you have to shell acorns. The shell is hard enough to prevent peeling but pliant enough to defeat actual cracking.

I ended up using crab crackers, semi-cracking and semi-peeling the acorns to get to the nut meat. This took hours for the three or four pounds of acorns I gathered from my friend's lawn. It is hard on the fingernails and fingertips.

Subsequent research revealed that if you boil the acorns very briefly, the shell is much easier to remove. But the patience it took to shell them was nothing compared to the patience it took to leach them.

Every acorn is high in tannic acid. That is why their juice has traditionally been used to cure hides. The tannic acid is very bitter. Eating an unleached acorn is like trying to eat an uncured olive. Don't!

The tannic acid is water-soluble. The Native Americans put baskets of shelled acorns in streams with running water. After weeks of leaching, the acid was washed out. My method was recommended in *Acorns and Eat'em*, by Suellen Ocean, 1993, Ocean-House, which, along with *It Will Live Forever*, by Beverly R. Ortiz and Julia F. Parker, 1991, Heyday Books, are the two best works on the subject that I could find locally.

I chopped the acorns into split pea size in my food processor. Then I put the chopped acorns into a large glass jar and covered them with water.

I changed the water every day for nearly a month. Finally, the nuts had lost their acidity. I was tempted to add lye after the first week, as we do with olives, but wanted to remain true to the traditional methods, at least for a while.

I then returned the acorns to the food processor and reduced them to a corn meal consistency. I drained the mash, poured it out onto a cookie sheet, and put it into the oven on the lowest setting overnight to dry the water out of the meal.

In the morning, I had a nicely dried-out product that I had to process one more time to make it a consistent meal.

Once I had convinced my family that acorns were not on the list of WMDs, and were both edible and delicious (at least that is what the books said), I prepared them to consume.

Since the acorn meal looked like polenta, I boiled it in water flavored with granulated chicken broth. After twenty minutes of cooking the resulting mush was delicious. It was sweet and nutty.

That's when I decided I had to give the mush the ultimate test. I (don't tell my doctor about this) fried patties of the mush in bacon fat until the outside was crisp. Oh my God! Talk about a little slice of heaven.

Acorns are a little trouble, but they are so central to life around us, and so darn good, that it'd be a shame if you didn't try them once.

BANANA SLUGS

Y ou know you must really be on to something when everyone's first comment is "You're not really going to eat that!"

"Well," says I, "as a matter of fact, I am intending to eat it . . . the banana slug that is."

If you spend any time whatsoever in the woods around Cloverdale, or, even better, at the coast, you are familiar with banana slugs. They are those very large yellow, green, brown, and black blobs that ooze their way out of the foliage and onto lawns, paths, and decks.

Banana slugs are mollusks, just like abalone . . . so they must be good, right?

The Pacific Banana Slug is the second-largest species of terrestrial slug in the world. Some grow to nearly ten inches long. They live in moist areas and feed on leaves, animal droppings, and dead plant material. They excrete nitrogen-rich fertilizer. Pretty handy guys to have around in a forest.

What is somewhat off-putting, except I guess if you are another banana slug, is the slimy mucus that banana slugs secrete all over themselves. This mucus coating helps keep the banana slugs hydrated and slows down the other critters that like to eat them like raccoons and skunks.

Banana slugs are modern lovers. They are hermaphrodites. When they mate, they pass sperm to their partner, then each slug lays eggs, from which they both run and never look back. By run, I'm talking about the six-and-a-half inches they can move per minute.

Besides being the mascot of the University of California at Santa Cruz, banana slugs were a favorite food of the Yurok tribe whose range included the downstream portion of the Klamath River in Northern California.

At a recent abalone camp, I set about to see what kind of food the slugs would make. It's not easy finding banana slug recipes but, I did locate a website that suggested soaking them in vinegar to remove the slime. Figuring, what with my familiarity with abalone, how hard could it be to cook a slug.

The hard part turned out trying to find slugs. The camp on the coast at Little River should have had an overflow of slugs. It was heavily forested and constantly wet from the marine layer. However, after an hour of searching, and turning up only one slug, I resorted to my secret weapon: ten-year-olds.

What kid wouldn't get completely excited about a contest involving the collection of banana slugs? Well, being as I was camped with a group of other lawyers, their children and grandchildren were not the highly spontaneous types. However, for a bounty of fifty cents a slug, they got interested really quickly.

I soon ended up with fifteen or twenty six-inch slugs that I stored in a used pizza box. When I went around to collect the slugs in the late afternoon, they'd eaten the top layer of cardboard off the pizza box. My kind of slugs.

The recipe goes like this: Cover the slugs with vinegar. This both kills them and loosens their slime. Let them soak for fifteen minutes. Run the slugs under cold water until all the slime is gone. Cut off their heads and run your thumb up their stomachs to extrude their innards. Slice the slugs vertically making rings. Then, think snails!

Out comes the garlic, parsley, olive oil, butter, salt, and pepper. Put some olive oil in a sauté pan and let it heat. Add the butter and let it foam. Then add the garlic and cook for about fifteen seconds, then add the snails and parsley. Cook for a minute or two. Season to taste with the salt and pepper.

Believe it or not, these guys are delicious. They are as good as any escargot I've ever eaten. (Of course, just about anything with enough butter, garlic, and parsley is going to be good to eat.)

So, here's to the lowly banana slug, washed down with a chilled Sauvignon Blanc.

BERRIES

I t's a love/hate thing. I love wild berries/I hate thorns!

Now that the rains have come, and the ground-scroungers are poking the forest duff for edible fungi, I guess it's safe to talk about the other summer foraging opportunity in Sonoma without putting my own secret patches at risk: Berries.

The hills and valleys around Cloverdale are a treasure trove of wild, and not-so-wild, berries.

The ubiquitous blackberry that seems to sprout up along every fence-line in the county is not a native plant. While there are eleven members of the blackberry family growing wild in California, the most common, the Himalayan blackberry is a Eurasian import.

Blackberries are not actually a true fruit. They are an aggregate fruit composed of small drupelets. Blackberries have biennial canes and perennial roots. If you have them on your property, and try to eliminate them, the term "perennial" takes on a whole new meaning. These guys are tough.

The native blackberries, thimbleberry, for instance, are much smaller than the Himalayan and produce much less fruit. The thimbleberry and its native sisters are, however, important modern food and shelter sources for herbivores and omnivores like squirrels, raccoons, and bears.

Blackberries are most often found near a reliable source of groundwater and old homesteads. Anthropological studies show that humans have been eating blackberries for many thousands of years. Their canes take two years to produce fruit. They produce thorns the first year! That's an ornery plant.

The local Pomo people ate serviceberries, gooseberries,

salmonberries, salal berries, wild strawberries, raspberries, thimbleberries, elderberries, black and purple nightshade berries, and huckleberries.

Serviceberry shrubs are deciduous with alternate leaves, lower side paler than upper, and are oval in shape. The leaf edges are scalloped. The bush blooms with white flowers between April and June and the berries, small and red are in clusters at the end of branches. The Pomo ate the berries fresh while other tribes mashed them to an edible paste or dried them to store. Serviceberries are usually found on dry, rock slopes.

Gooseberries, both "thorny" and "smooth," were collected during the late spring and summer by tribes all over California. The thorny berries were rubbed in a collecting basket to remove the spines that cover the fruit before they were eaten. The smooth gooseberries were eaten off the bush. Northern California tribes, including the Pomo and Hupa, also dried the fruit, as they did with most all other berries, made a dry pulp, and mixed the pulp with meat to make pemmican.

The Pomo basket makers designed special baskets to collect the fruit and to winnow out husks and loose seeds from the final product.

Thorny gooseberries look like round red sea urchins with their spines sticking out at every angle. The smooth berries have much less thorny protection. Gooseberries are generally located on dry slopes.

Huckleberries are a fabulous treat that are most often collected at the coast. If you look back through the Douglas firs and redwoods on the hillsides above the coastline, you can see the huckleberry bushes crowded together and standing three or four feet high. The leaves are oval-shaped and have small teeth on their edges but, *no thorns*!

Huckleberries are just good eating. You can use them like a blueberry and eat them fresh or bake them into bread.

A great favorite of the Pomo was the wild grape. Although the pre-European wild grapes are not as sweet as the wine and table grapes we are used to, the local tribes made jams and juice drinks out of them. According to Margaret Dubin and Sara-Larus Tolley, whose *Seaweed, Salmon, and Manzanita Cider . . . A California Indian Feast* (2008, Heyday Books) is a beautiful and authoritative work, wild grapes were also used as bait in bird traps, and to catch fish, crabs, and octopus.

Wild strawberries grow along the foggy coast but it's rare that you can find enough of them in a day to cover your Wheaties. Look for them on bluffs above the beach or deep in the redwood stands of Del Norte county.

The nice thing about berries is that, even as the blood flows from a good thorn stick, gobbling down a mouthful of them is sweet revenge.

BIRDING

Over the years, it's been called to my attention (primarily by readers who hold that the devil has a special place for bird-murder'n duck hunters), that there's more to the outdoors than trying to decide which bird species goes good with plum sauce (most do! But I digress).

As much as I do love chasing and eating game, there really is a lot to be said for bird watching. There, I said it . . . satisfied? Much waterfowl hunting actually consists of little more than extended periods of bird watching so I'm pretty practiced in it.

For the serious birder, though, the month of January is the absolute peak time to get out into the field. Most birders have what they call their "life list." This is no more than a list of birds that they have seen and identified. In January there is no better place to fill out chunks of a life list than the Sacramento Valley and, specifically, the Sacramento National Wildlife Refuge near Willows.

The end of December, and the beginning of January, mark the high point of the annual waterfowl migration. The Sacramento Refuge is one of a series of refuges set up in the Sacramento Valley. One of the justifications for the creation of the refuge system was the insistence of rice farmers in the northern valley that migrating waterfowl must be controlled to protect the rice crop. The farmers persuaded the Federal Government to create the refuges rather than have the farmers take care of the problem on their own, i.e., eliminate the problem ducks and geese.

The Sacramento Refuge is about two hours and twenty minutes from Cloverdale. Take Highway 20 to Williams, then go north on Interstate 5, about ten minutes, to Road 68, the Princeton Road. Go east to old Highway 99 and turn left. The refuge is about a mile and a half north.

At the refuge, there is a visitor's center and lots of printed information. The refuge is unique because from the visitor's center you can drive through a portion of the refuge on a well-maintained, six-mile-long gravel road. The road winds through the restored marsh areas of the refuge and permits close-up observation of three hundred species of birds and mammals. Admission is free!

During the winter, the refuge holds three million migrating ducks and one million geese!

Armed with a good field guide, like Roger Tory Peterson's *A Field Guide To Western Birds* (which includes a life list check-off page), and a good pair of binoculars, you can pull over most anywhere along the road and see mallards, sprig, green wing, blue wing and cinnamon teal, gadwall, canvasback, shovelers (spoonbills), golden eye, bufflehead, widgeon, red heads, mud hens, Canada geese, white-fronted geese (specklebelly), snow geese, Ross's geese, cackling geese, and tule geese, and, maybe, a sand hill crane.

There are herons, cranes, pheasant, and huge flocks of white face ibis. There are enough shorebirds, from curlew to snipe, to fill out a page of a life list. There are dozens of raptors and owls, including marsh hawks, red tail and red shoulder hawks, coopers hawks, kestrels, and golden and bald eagles. The marsh also teams with resident and migratory songbirds, too numerous to mention.

At sunrise and sunset, you have a great chance to see coyotes, skunks, raccoons, beavers, muskrats, minks, deer, bobcats, and a whole host of small weasel-type critters.

About halfway through the drive, which can be completed in as little as twenty minutes if you are in a hurry, is an observation platform that gets you above the tules and bull rush, and permits a panoramic view of the refuge. The platform is a great place for lunch.

There are lots of places to eat and stay in Willows, about five miles up I-5. On the return trip, there are a couple of interesting ways to go west, back to Highway 101. One road goes from Willows, past Black Butte Lake, and over the mountains into Covelo. Another goes from Williams, around the north end of Indian Valley Lake, and to Nice through Bartlett Springs. Both roads are good gravel paths, but sometimes, sloppy when wet. If you take Highway 20, you have a better than even chance of seeing some of the elk that inhabit eastern Lake and western Colusa Counties.

BLACK BASS

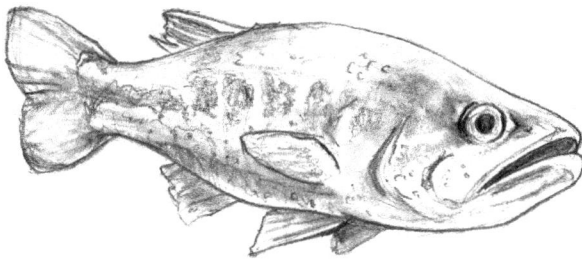

The look on Chet's face as the huge bass exploded four feet out of the greenish water was, as it goes in the commercial, "priceless." For the next five minutes, Chet hyperventilated, swore, prayed, and generally made pleading conversation with a fish that bent his rod down like a horseshoe.

After the fish tired, and Chet was able to guide it toward his boat, I got a lucky pinch on its lower jaw and lifted the monster onto the casting deck. I didn't think peoples' eyes could actually enlarge as wide as Chet's orbs as he looked at the digital scale from which the fish hung. Ten pounds! Chet's all-time fish.

Out came the camera phone and digital camera for at least two dozen pictures before the fish went into the live well where it was kept cool and comfortable in flowing oxygenated water. Then came the excited cellphone calls to fishing buddies (including his fish-widow wife) announcing the catch and showing the prize via camera phone.

All this from a normally reasonable man. Thus is the lure of largemouth bass fishing.

The fish, a female, was released, as are 95 percent of the largemouth that are caught by devoted bass fishermen. This is catch-and-release fishing at its spiritual core.

Florida strain largemouth bass are not, as you might deduce from the name, native to California. In fact, there are no species of bass native to California. The group of fish known as "black bass," as distinguished from striped bass, include largemouth, smallmouth, and spotted bass.

Largemouth were first imported from Quincy, Illinois, in 1891. The Florida largemouth arrived in 1959. Smallmouth bass were first introduced from Lake Champlain, New York, in 1874. Spotted bass are a more recent addition to the California scene, having arrived from Alabama in 1974.

All black bass are fierce fighters and inhabit lakes, rivers, creeks, and the sloughs of the California Delta. Lake Sonoma holds all three strains of black bass, but the queen of Northern California bass waters is Clear Lake.

Fishermen, male and female, come from across the nation, and overseas, to Clear Lake to tackle some of the biggest bass ever recorded. Springtime is the height of bass season. This is when the bass pair up, make beds like nests where they hatch, and raise their young for a month or so. Generally, the smaller males will guard the bed while the females forage. However, both male and female bass are insanely protective of their beds. This makes for sensational fishing.

Bass are generally taken with lures. There is an industry rivaling the auto industry devoted to bass lures. They go from simple plastic worms, to crank baits that imitate bait fish, to spinner baits that don't appear to imitate anything, to surface poppers and plastic frogs, and back again in an array of colors and patterns that would make Jackson Pollack blush.

Truly, half the business of bass fishing is in fretting over the right lure. The completely devoted tend to look for bass in excess of ten pounds. To catch these, the Clearlake fishermen use rubber trout lures nine inches long (which is bigger than most of the trout I've caught in my lifetime!). My friend Chet carries the equivalent of a medium tackle shop with him in his boat at all times. You just never know what lure will be working.

And don't get me started on the boats!

In addition to its obsession with fishing tackle, the tournament bass fishing industry is compulsive about its boats. The theory here, or at least the justification they give their wives in order to purchase these monsters, is that you have to get to the hot spots before your competition. This involves low-slung boats that are routinely powered by motors larger than 250 horsepower and which fly over, not through, the water in excess of eighty miles per hour. And they aren't cheap.

The boats are basically casting platforms with enough storage to hold all the tackle one could ever consider using. They have electric auxiliary motors to help sneak up on fish and live wells, with continuous fresh water movement, to store fish until they can be weighed and released.

A professional bass fisherman can make a very good living traveling from tournament to tournament. The pros have lure and boat manufacturers as sponsors. It is not unusual for a tournament winner to be awarded a $60,000 bass boat, in addition to cash, as his or her prize.

As much as I respect catch-and-release fishing, and I do release most of the bass I catch, I will, from time to time, keep a fish to eat. I do this exclusively at Lake Shasta where the very cold temperature of the lake keeps the meat of the spotted bass sweet and tasty. My favorite Shasta Breakfast is a plate of bass filets, dipped in an egg wash and rolled in breadcrumbs, and then fried in leftover bacon fat. Oh man!

CLAMS

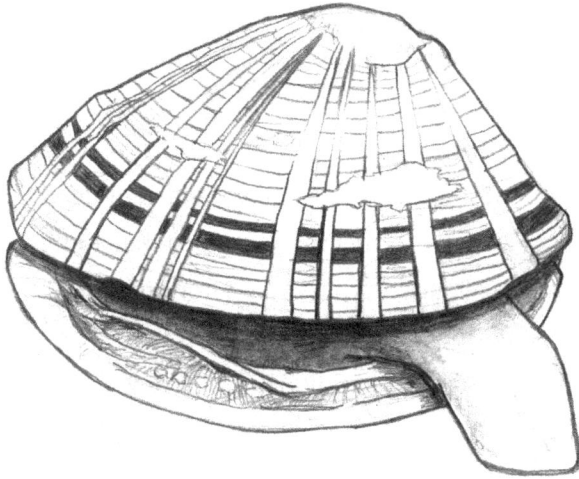

I t's time for the dirty work . . . or should I say, the child's play.

The lowest tides of the year occur in April. This is important because if abalones have gone beyond your reach, or ability to hold your breath, or if you have the blessing of small children, you should consider clam digging. But be advised, this is not a sport for the neat and clean set.

Clams like mud. Kids like mud. You can see where this is going.

The lowest tides of the year, the minus tides, can be over a foot lower than any other low tide of the year. That additional foot means that portions of the sea bottom that are not seen all year, all of a sudden pop out into view. It's time to find clams.

Clams are another of the forager's quarry that don't run very fast. That's a good thing if the forager doesn't run very fast, which is not an untypical condition. In fact, clams don't run at all, and, contrary to popular belief, they don't even swim very fast, or at all. By and large, clams get in the mud and stay there. The trick is to figure out where they are resting. (Why they would rest after doing nothing all day is a question my mother would ask . . . and has.)

Tomales Bay, Bodega Bay, and Humbolt Bay (do you see a pattern here?) are places for clams to rest . . . and for people to rest too for that matter. Where, in these idyllic locations, one looks for clams to forage depends on the kind of clam you wish to consume.

Here, the forager has several choices. Our local bays contain gaper clams, which are known as horseneck clams, Washington clams, cockles–which you see in the stores as steamers–and geoducks. Each type of clam has a different general type of habitat. The cockles like mud that is under, and mixed with, gravel and small cobbles. The horsenecks and Washingtons like mud that is mixed with sand.

By its simplest description, clam digging is no more than finding where a clam is resting and digging it up. Like most apparently simple things, this is more complicated than it appears.

Hunting cockles is hit or miss. They don't give their position away, so you need to look for a likely bed and start digging. Cockles do not live terribly far under the seafloor. You rarely have to dig more than a foot to eighteen inches to find them. Once you find one, you will likely find more. You can keep fifty cockles, but they must be at least one and one-half inches in greatest diameter.

I don't know if it still works, but it used to be that a Gerber baby food top made a pretty good cockle caliper, it being one and one-half inches in diameter. Not having needed baby food in the recent past, or, hopefully, in the near future, I can't tell you for sure.

The larger clams tend to be a bit more problematic to gather. Washingtons, which are smallish, are fairly easy to gather once you find a spot where they are located, as they do not lay too deep in the mud. Horsenecks and geoducks, the big clams are, however, another story.

The big clams live deep in the sand-mud, sometimes over three feet down. That being the case you do not want to just start digging and hope that there is a clam around. Way too much work! But the big clams are worth the dig since they provide much more meat than do the smaller clams.

The theory of finding the big clams is to wander the tidal flats until you see a clam spouting. The big clams have lots of meat because they live deep in the mud and extend their neck to the seafloor. This neck can mean a stretch of edible muscle over three feet long. The clams feed and circulate oxygenated water through the neck. Their wastewater looks like a small geyser when it is forced out of the end of the neck and out of the tidal mud.

The clam is not usually directly under the geyser. They tend to extend their neck at an angle and, at the first indication of a predator, like your footsteps on the mud, the clam will retract its neck back into its hole.

Many of the old-timers have wooden or metal rods that they gently wiggle down the hole the clam's neck makes until they feel it hit the clam's shell. This is akin to safe-cracking for the delicacy of touch it requires, but it doesn't take too long to master.

Once the clam is located, all you have to do is dig it out. This is much like St. Augustine trying to fill a hole in the beach with the water from the sea–except in reverse. Typically, every shovel full of mud you dig out of a hole in a tidal flat is replaced very quickly with fresh wet sand-mud, compliments of the surrounding sand-mud.

To get around this rule of nature (who, remember, abhors a vacuum), you need to shore the hole. This is usually done with a section of two-foot diameter, or larger, ABS conduit, cut about three feet long. As will be apparent below, it helps to have cut handles at one end of the conduit or attach rope handles.

Another valuable tool for the clam digger is a slurp gun. This is like a big hypodermic needle that will pull sand-mud out of your hole in the mud by suction. You can actually buy these PVC creations at some sports stores if you call around. A small-bladed shovel is also a requirement.

Once you find the clam and mark its location, you set the conduit above the likely resting place of the clam and work it down into the sand-mud. Then you start digging and sucking sand out of the hole.

As you get deeper, work the conduit down into the hole to prevent the sides from collapsing and filling your hole.

If you figured right, you should be able to work your hand down into the final inches of sand-mud and feel the clam. Then all you have to do is jiggle it loose from its surroundings and pull the little bugger out. You also have to pull your conduit out, thus the handles.

Needless to say, if you are really working hard enough to actually get a clam, you will be covered with sand-mud from head to toe.

This is where kids come in. You probably have never seen the look of utter amazement and delight on a kid's face (usually little boys but most little girls will succumb to this as well) when you say that it is ok to get as muddy as you want. In fact, it may change their entire approach to life, and you, when you encourage them to help out by playing in the mud.

The limit on horsenecks and Washingtons is ten of each species (fifty in Humbolt Bay). You must keep every gaper or Washington clam you dig up regardless of size. The geoduck limit is three and you must keep every one you dig up.

During periods of red tide, usually in the summer, you may not take clams as their consumption is potentially lethal owing to the toxins produced by the red tide plankton. Check with Fish and Game or most fishing stores to see if there is a quarantine in place.

When you get clams home, put them in fresh water for about four hours. They will spit out much of the sand that they have ingested. The freshwater bath will also loosen the tough skin that covers the horseneck's neck and permit its easy removal.

Cockles are easy to cook. Steam them over white wine loaded with garlic, parsley, and butter. They are cooked when they open.

Dump any clams that don't open. My favorite way to eat steamers is to just pull the cooked clam out of its shell with a fork and dip it into the cooked wine and herbs. A chunk of French bread in the liquid is not awful either.

The horsenecks make great chowder. Mince the necks and portions of white meat from inside the shell. Dump the dark portions of the clam.

A basic chowder starts with thin slices of salt pork, chopped up and fried until mostly rendered. Fry a chopped-up onion in the pork fat and add a little minced garlic after the onions are transparent. Pour in a couple of bottles of clam juice and boil for twenty minutes or a half-hour with a bay leaf and whatever vegetable you like in your chowder. I like sweet red peppers and celery. Traditionally, you also add cubed potatoes, but I've found that if you want to keep the starch down, and make a lighter chowder, you can use chopped-up cauliflower instead. You can add white wine if you want to make a bisque. Salt and pepper to taste.

Add the clams for five minutes then add a cube of butter and a pint of heavy cream. Bring the chowder back to temperature but don't boil it. Heaven.

CRAWDADS

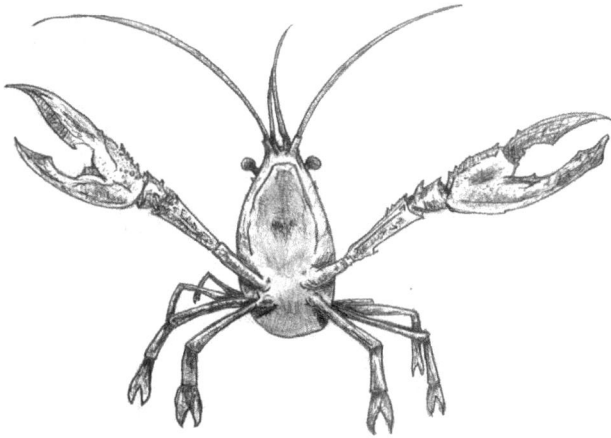

Whew ... hot! Cloverdale hot! Not much daytime foraging in this weather ... until the deer season opens.

It's time for crayfish, crawdads, mud bugs, or summer shrimp. Whatever you call them, these little buggers are the reason I forage. The Russian River is full of them, and they are easy and fun to get. Crawdads feed a wide variety of riverine critters from herons and raccoons to smallmouth bass and coyotes. They are, in fact, delicious, tasting much like a very sweet shrimp.

Catching crawdads is simple and fun. When I was a kid vacationing on Austin Creek, I'd dive under the willow roots with a face mask and fins and grab the bugs by hand. Little kids, and big kids too, can spend an enormously entertaining day just walking along the channel side of the river and dropping a piece of bacon tied to a kite string into the places where rocks slow down the river flow. The crawdads tend to stay in the slow water.

The crawdads are such tenacious eaters that once they latch on to the bacon with their pincers, they won't usually let go until they've been pulled from the water. If you have a little net, you can scoop them before they let go.

For the lazy, including me, a simple crawdad trap left in the river overnight will usually produce a meal of dads. The easiest trap to build is no more than a two-foot or three-foot tube made out of quarter-inch hardware cloth that you can get at the hardware store. Make the tube with a ten-inch to one-foot diameter. Fashion funnels from the hardware cloth that have the same diameter as the trap on their big end and about a two-inch diameter at the little end.

You wire the funnels onto the ends of the tube, pointing into the trap. The crawdads can easily walk in but have a hard time trying to find a way out. Cut a flap in the side of the trap so you can bait it.

You can bait the traps with about any kind of oily meat, preferably something the dads can't tear apart and walk away with. I use a can of cheap cat food with holes in it. Cat food is pretty smelly and, with only a little of it disappearing each night through small holes in the can, one can last several nights.

Tie a rope to the trap and throw it into slow water along the edge of the river. Tie off the rope to a tree so you can retrieve the trap. You can trap dads anytime, but I think they are more active at night, so I set traps in the evening and retrieve the crawdads in the morning.

Over at the duck club, in the Central Valley, which masquerades as a rice ranch most of the year, we wait until the rice is just about ripe. That's when the farmer pulls the water off the rice and thousands of crawdads are confined to a relatively small number of deep spots. We use traps and casting nets to harvest them. Just about any slowly moving slough or ditch in the Valley will hold lots of crawdads.

Crawdads are best cooked live. Since they hibernate during the winter, crawdads' metabolism is adjustable and slows way down in the cold. If you cover crawdads with ice as soon as you catch them, they will stay alive for days.

Eating crawdads is as much fun as catching them. Wash them well to get off any mud. Start a big pot of water boiling and add to it a crab boil (pronounced "crab ball" in Louisiana). Zatarain's makes a great crab boil and you can usually get it at Ray's Market. Otherwise, just throw in a bunch of bay leaves, salt, black pepper, and chile peppers into the boiling water. Hot and salty is good.

Boil the dads for about five minutes. Drain them and pour them out onto a table covered with newspaper. Then go to work. Break off the tails and peel them. Dip them in a little butter, lemon, or anything that tickles your tongue. Real aficionados suck out the contents of the crawdad head. It's a Southern thing–don't ask. When you're done, just fold up the newspaper, and the dishes are done.

DEER HUNTING

Ralph Mendez pretty well summed it up for me one afternoon while we were taking a jeep ride around the hunting ranch.

"Deer hunting," he said, "is ten percent actually looking for deer, eighty percent cooking, eating, card playing, storytelling (some truthful, others not so), dice shaking, arguing politics, comparing sports teams, bragging about dogs, generally hanging out in camp, and ten percent . . . drinking beer." (In Ralph's case, the last category may be slightly understated . . . but who's counting.)

On the second Saturday of August each year, the tribe's men leave the comfort of home and hearth and, like their ancestors, take to the hills to rustle up some food. For most deer hunters in Sonoma County, their destinations are pretty standard: camps under trees, furnished with ancient spring beds, set up outside under tin-roofed, open-sided sheds, screened-in cooking areas armed with enormous Wolf ranges, and screened-in skinning sheds.

Some camps actually have indoor eating or cooking areas, but not many. The theory here is to commune with nature . . . and avoid unnecessary tidying up. Suffice to say, there are very few regular female residents of Sonoma County's deer camps.

But hunt we do, with varying success, depending on the year. The primary method of deer hunting in Sonoma County relies on a group of younger, fitter, hunters who enter the thick brush, at either the top of a canyon or, as the old Italians did it, at the bottom of a canyon. These individuals, known affectionately as the "walkers," "doggers," or just "dogs," climb noisily through the brush, sometimes in the company of real dogs, in an attempt to make male deer reluctantly leave their day-time hiding places.

Other individuals, those of us who have attained seniority by virtue of age and infirmity, though not necessarily hunting skill, take up locations along the line of the hunt, known as stands, with an eye toward shooting any deer foolish enough to leave the heavy cover of oak, madrone, or chemise.

The term "stand" is a disingenuous description because most of us "standers," owing to our aforementioned age or infirmities, tend to sit on a stand. (You have to be there to see the beauty in this oxymoron.)

The hunters on the stands identify the location of the walkers by listening to the distinctive hoot, or call, of each dogger as he moves through the brush. This protects the walkers from being misidentified as particularly slow deer and also tends to promote keeping the stand-keepers awake.

Another venerable method of hunting deer, generally looked down upon by purists, is the road hunt.

After lunch and a nap, most camps break up into groups and mount four-wheel-drive vehicles. The jeeps drive the roads that crisscross the ranches looking for deer who will frequently move from one hiding place to another during the afternoon. Sometimes, a good road hunt is the only way any of us ever see a deer. This is surprising, considering the fact that most road hunts are distinguished by a constant chatter amongst the hunters over every topic that did not get completely exhausted at the lunch table.

In the end, most camps find some success, and deer are taken to the skinning shed to be processed. The skinned, cleaned carcasses are split and air-dried until the weekend is over, and they are returned to finish hanging in walk-in refrigerators.

Deer need to be cleaned and cooled as soon as possible after they are shot, and then left to hang in the open air of a refrigerated container for at least one week to be edible. I mean, you can eat them sooner, but you will hear people talk about "gaminess" if the deer aren't cared for properly.

Truly, the best part about deer camp is the food. I have had the great fortune to have been taught camp cooking by some masters. Ray Seghesio is probably the best camp cook I've ever met. Babe Zanzi also taught me a lot about feeding hunters in an outdoor camp. Currently, I am graced with the incredible preparations of Scott Cavallo and Dave Ciapucsi.

Good, Italian-based camp food always includes a salad, with tuna (unless the aforementioned Ralph Mendez is present), pasta–with tomato gravy that is made during the early summer and stored frozen in milk cartons–and French bread.

Perhaps the best meal includes a well-aged venison ham sliced into quarter-inch to half-inch steaks. The steaks are gently pounded to tenderize them. Eggs are whipped up and the steaks take an egg bath. They are then dredged in bread crumbs and fried in a mixture of olive oil and butter. The steaks are quickly cooked and, after receiving a light "baptism" of white wine, removed from the heat while they are still very pink at their center. Like any game. **DON'T OVER COOK THEM!** A squeeze of lemon at the table finishes off morsels that melt in your mouth and remind you why you still hunt deer.

DOVES

Come sunrise, on the first of September, the hills are feeling just the slightest hint of the approaching fall. The air is soft, and still a little humid from the last days of August.

In the Central Valley of California, the air is pungent with the perfume of freshly cut alfalfa and hay. In Cloverdale, on the gravel bars that line the Russian River, the first mayflies of the day are rising and the river is giving off its last fragrances of a long summer.

This is the day the dove hunters gather to open the new season. They huddle in groups of two to twenty, having a last cup of coffee from a thermos or fiddling with their decoys, shotguns, or shells. Stories are told about last year's opener, or that great opener twenty years ago in Arizona or Mexico.

The hunters disburse to their share of the field or gravel bar, usually behind what little cover may be allowed them in a swath of cut safflower, sunflowers, alfalfa, or river willows. Dove decoys are pinned to tree branches or set to spinning on stakes in the earth.

And then . . . the wait.

The first doves come slipping through when there is not quite enough light to make a good shot. Singles and pairs. Darting and dipping at astounding speed, even in good light, you wonder if you could have gotten off a shot. The sound of the wind in their wings is distinctive and brings the hair on your neck to attention.

Finally, if they haven't shot this particular field before, the hunters strain to identify where the birds were roosting last night, and gauge their path to their first food and water of the morning.

Doves will follow straight lines to food and water. Power lines, roads, canals, rivers, tree lines, and fence lines are all magnets for doves. The secret is to identify the straight-line features early and position yourself under the flight path.

The first substantial flocks of doves follow the early-birds moments later, as do the blackbirds. On opening day the brain's muscle memory, the recognition of a dove's flight pattern versus a blackbird's flight, clicks in pretty quickly, permitting one to identify the difference between birds at a hundred yards, give or take, depending on the age of your eyes.

Then the first shots are fired, and the barrage begins. All around you shotguns are firing, doves are falling, and dogs are racing to retrieve them. Hunters are calling to each other: "Behind you," "Coming right at you," "Over you," and "Great shot!"

Then it's quiet. The first flocks have passed and have experienced enough noise and chaos to quickly put them on their guard for the rest of the day. Panting dogs are given a quick drink and panting hunters take whatever refreshment they have brought with them to the field.

As the day settles in, the occasional flock or single dove flies the gauntlet and draws multiple shots. If anything, after the sun has shown itself fully, the doves fly even more erratically, if that is possible.

Dead birds are quickly plucked and put on ice. And then it's usually time for breakfast.

Statistically, dove hunting is the most popular hunting sport in the United States. That may not be apparent in Sonoma County, but if you get out to the Midwest or the South on the first of September, you can watch one of the great American social events.

Across the country, families assemble for the dove opener. Because you can hunt doves with shotguns from small .410-gauge weapons up to large 12-gauge guns, both kids and women can handily participate.

The popularity of dove hunting stems from a variety of factors. There are a lot of doves. Owing to modern hunting regulations, the dove population in the United States, and particularly in the State of California, is very stable. Doves, being a migratory bird, travel from Canada and the United States to Mexico and Central America each year. Consequently, hunting them is regulated by Federal Law and international treaty.

In Northern California, three species of doves are available for hunting, mourning doves, white-winged doves, and the newly arrived Eurasian collared dove. Typically, Sonoma County hunters see mourning doves and Eurasian doves, as white-winged doves tend to stay in the southern desert areas.

The limit on mourning doves and white-winged doves is ten birds per day and, after opening day, twenty doves in possession. Neither the Federal Fish and Wildlife Agency, nor the California Department of Fish and Game have set limits on Eurasian collared doves. The Eurasians have only been a local phenomenon for the last ten years, and nobody seems to know much about them. The Eurasians have taken over Sonoma County and seem to stay here all year. Mourning doves migrate south beginning in late August.

It only takes a relatively light weather front to cue the birds into heading south so you can pretty much set your watch by the fact that there is be a little front pass through Sonoma County about a week before the dove season starts. Never fails!

The Pomo used woven traps to take doves, probably because hitting a dove with a bow and arrow is a quick way to lose a lot of arrows and not get much meat. They used the same traps to catch woodpeckers. The traps were much like fish traps, funnels that permit the bird to enter but not turn around to quickly get out of the trap.

Some of my favorite dove memories are of the Mexican housekeepers at the Arizona motel where my buddies and I would stay to shoot in the desert on opening day. In Arizona, you must stop dove hunting at noon. By the time we returned to our motel for a swim and a beer the ladies were just getting off their morning shift. For a trade of doves, and not a lot of money, the ladies would take our doves, marinate them, and return in the evening, with their husbands and kids, and barbeque the birds on the motel lawn. We all shared the birds with tortillas and more beer.

My favorite recipe for doves is to split them down the back and spread them. Then they go into a marinade of tequila, lime, and chiles for a couple of hours, then barbequed until they are just rare. Many of my friends make a rich gravy and pour it over roasted doves. Either way, the little birds are absolutely delicious.

DUCKS

W e assemble an hour before the first light will show over the Sierra Foothills to the east. It's usually frosty, if not downright frigid. Occasionally, the weather approaches monsoonish.

The six or eight members who will hunt today move in and out of the cargo container: the duck club's "headquarters."

In the warmth of the container, blind assignments are confirmed and games of "high card" are played for blinds left vacant by members who decided to sleep in on this blustery Saturday morning.

Jibes are traded over yesterday's missed shots. Friends ask after each other's families. Dogs pant, jump, and scurry in excitement; they are ready to go.

The club is getting ready for a new day in the marsh.

Finally, the hunters gather up their equipment: packs, guns, coffee, food, and decoys and start their march in the dark for the blinds.

Since it depends so heavily on machinery, automatic shotguns, and mechanically powered moving decoys, most people wouldn't consider modern duck hunting to be foraging, per se.

To the local Native Americans, especially those who lived closer to the Bay, ducks were a staple, especially during the winter migrations that saw millions of ducks enter California from the north.

The locals netted and shot ducks with arrows from brush blinds after luring them into range with decoys made out of tules. Not completely unlike modern duck hunters.

Duck hunting is less about hunting than it is about luring. More than any other kind of foraging, hunting ducks is a psychological exercise that requires the hunter to think like a duck and communicate like a duck. Ducks are highly social birds. Unlike fishing, where you lure fish with the promise of food (bait), ducks are lured by the promise of company–other ducks.

The fun in duck hunting is in the preparation. Duck decoys are as old an art form as cave drawings. They can be so detailed that the exact number of feathers are painted on the block. Or they can be as simple as a white rag on a stick or a slice of old tire.

The fun is in setting out a string of decoys that looks like a resting flock to birds flying above. They can't be set too close to each other because, while ducks like other ducks, they don't like to be crowded. You need to leave the ducks an open spot in the decoy spread where they can land. They don't like to fly closely over other ducks. The spread has to say, "Here is safety in numbers."

Calling ducks from a blind is what the sport is about. To see a pair of ducks hundreds of yards away, know that they are looking for a place to land, and then make sounds with a duck call that draws them to you is the essence of the hunt.

Effective duck calling requires knowing a dozen different calls (specific sound patterns) made with two or three different calls (sound-making devices). But the art of it is to know when to use the "hailing call" versus the "lonely hen" call versus the "feeding chuckle." It takes years of sitting in blinds, watching how ducks behave, to learn how to communicate with them.

I say all this, but must admit that the best thing about duck hunting is the blinds. Most blinds are concrete, metal, or wooden tubs, sunken into the marsh, so that when you get in them and sit down, you are at eye level with the water and covered with brush or tules.

The scene from a duck blind is like no other. If you don't jump around and wave your arms a lot, the creatures who inhabit the marsh will ignore you, even if they see your head.

Watching the marsh wake up from a duck blind is like no other show in town. Each species has its time to appear. The ducks and geese returning from nighttime feeding are usually first. Then, as the light begins to show in the east, the owls return low over the water to their daytime roosts. The muskrats and beavers will usually take a quick look as they bed down for the day. Deer poke gracefully from marsh hillocks.

Blackbirds and ibis move like black clouds just off the tops of the tules. Finally, the big raptors, hawks, and eagles move into the sky to spend the day hunting the small rodents that scamper up to the blinds all day.

After years of thinking about it, I've determined that the most important thing about spending a day in a duck blind is the quality daydreaming. I don't think most people daydream enough. I know I don't get much of a chance to do it during the week. (Daydreaming while driving is prevalent, but not encouraged.)

The wonderful thing about being in a duck blind is that you tend to spend hour after hour looking at empty skies. There is absolutely nothing more conducive to a good daydream than an empty sky into which you are required to stare hour after hour. Guilt-free daydreaming . . . what a concept!

FROGS

The other diners in the Fall River fishing resort restaurant cast furtive glances our way as my two friends and I eased our way out the back door of the lodge and into the gently bobbing rowboat.

The looks we were getting had less to do with the fact that we were going out on a lake at 11:00 p.m., than with the collection of miners' headlights, diving lights, nets, gigs, and wine bottles with which we were arrayed.

At my insistence, we were going frogging after a very slow day of trout fishing.

With apologies to Dennis Matasci, of Cloverdale's Breaking New Ground Coffee Shop–who probably holds more Calaveras Jumping Frog championships than anyone in history–I must say, frogs, besides being great athletes, are just plain good to eat, and great fun to catch.

Bullfrogs inhabit freshwater streams and ponds all over California. The Sacramento/San Joaquin delta area probably has the most concentration of frogs in the state. In the Central Valley, irrigation canals and stock ponds are also fertile breeding grounds for frogs.

It has been noted, however, that the use of agricultural herbicides and pesticides in the Valley has impacted the frog populations. There are apparently not as many frogs as there use to be.

In Sonoma County, swampy areas adjacent to the Russian River, and the multitude of farm ponds and mill ponds scattered throughout the hills, hold good populations of bullfrogs. You know a good frog pond when you see industrial-size polliwogs scooting through the shallow edges of the pond during the day.

Springtime is usually the best time to find bullfrogs. Frogging is partially an auditory pursuit. The male bullfrog attracts females at night by making his rumbling bass croaks, over and over, until the poor addled females give up (probably just to preserve their sanity) and cozy up to the big guy. This is the time to locate the frogs by keying in on their call.

Since the hunt is done at night, you generally can't see the frogs that you hear until you put a light on them. It helps to have scouted the area in the daylight just to reduce the potential for getting in over your head . . . literally.

Some froggers like to hunt from float tubes, and some like canoes or prams. Some freaks like to get down in wetsuits and creep up on the frogs from the muck of the pond. I had a friend who wasn't content with diving lights. He hunted from an inner tube and dragged along with him another inner tube with a plywood platform tied on it, to which he attached a twelve-volt automobile battery and an automobile headlight. Man, you shine that baby on a frog, and he is lit up.

Once you have a light on the frog, the hard part starts. Catching big frogs by hand requires incredible stealth and patience. Frogs will rarely stick around while you are splashing toward them with oars flying. It usually requires two persons–one to hold the light to distract the frog, and one to reach around the frog from the rear to grab it with both hands.

You can also use nets. However, these usually get caught up in tules and tree branches. You can also use a frog gig, which is a broomstick diameter spear of varying lengths with a tri-prong or four-prong spearhead on it. These are not easy to use and take some practice.

Once you grab a frog, you will appreciate the fact that you brought a gunny sack to keep the frogs in. They are strong and quick to escape.

There is no limit on the number of bullfrogs you can take, but there are limits on all other frogs and amphibians. Frogs are game amphibians. You must have a fishing license in your possession to take them.

Frog legs, just the hind legs, are usually cooked like fried chicken. Skin the legs, roll them in seasoned flour, then an egg wash, then more flour. Or, soak them in buttermilk for an hour then roll them in seasoned flour. Fry the legs in butter and olive oil until browned and crisp. Serve the legs with a lemon wedge to squeeze over them.

Frog legs taste like (and you know this is coming) chicken. My father would say why not just eat chicken . . . but that's another whole debate.

That night on the Fall River pond, we saw lots of frogs, but never actually got one in the boat. Gradually, as it got later, and the wine bottles evaporated, we each nodded off to sleep until, with the sun rising, our other friends roused us for more trout fishing. It was the toughest morning of trout fishing I ever had . . . until about 9:00 a.m. . . . when I fell back to sleep . . . on the banks of the Fall River.

IN BETWEEN
TIME

With the exception of some hard-driven, frostbitten steelheaders, many foragers take to equipment cleaning and trip planning this time of year. However, the true forager knows that February can provide a wealth of gathering activities amidst relatively uncrowded conditions.

It's not that the fishing is out of the question. **Phil VanGelder** of Geyserville landed two bright hen steelhead below Miner Hole on the Gualala last week. Phil was using a red-head fly at the top of the tide. There are reports of native and hatchery fish throughout the Russian River system, but with clear water, and fair weather, spots like the mouth of Dry Creek are shoulder to shoulder. In fact, the old-timers say that on a good day you can walk across the parking lot on the backs of the anglers.

Depending on the weather (DOTW), crabbing this time of year provides a great chance for the forager to scratch his or her itch. A simple hoop net, available at most tackle shops, thrown off the Bodega breakwater will turn up the occasional Dungeness crab or, more readily, a rock crab. The Dungeness have to be five and three-quarters inches across their shell from in front of the eyes. Rock crabs only have to be four inches across. The limit on Dungeness is ten, while the rock crab limit is thirty-five. In flat weather, a small boat will easily get you to the outer bay at Bodega where the crabbing is sometimes great. Crab pots that you can set overnight and check the next day run about $160 fully rigged with line and float.

Any kind of meat bait will do but all crabs are fond of fish heads. Check at Lucas Wharf or the Tides, or Ray's Market for that matter, to see if they have any used heads for bait.

The Asian fishermen just steam their crabs, but nothing beats them boiled in a spicy Cajun "crab boil" like Zatarain's. The difference in taste between a live crab and one that has been sitting on ice in a grocery store is what gets the forager through the workweek.

One of the forager's favorite February pursuits, DOTW, is winter poke polling. During the late winter and early spring, monkey face and wolf eels come inshore to spawn. This is when they are accessible to the forager.

The poke pole is nothing more than an eight-foot to ten-foot pole (stout bamboo or aluminum conduit works great), to which a straightened coat hanger is affixed. The end of the coat hanger is bent into a loop and a hook and short leader are attached. The best bait is cut squid, but whole shrimp work well.

Wait for a minus tide and wade out into the tide pools. "Poke" your bait well back under the exposed rocks and hold on. If you get an eel, it's best to just cut the leader while holding the eel in a gunny sack. Tying a new hook and leader is easier than un-hooking a moving eel no matter how much your buddies may enjoy watching you and the eel dance on seaweed-covered rocks.

Actually, anywhere along the coast where the minus tide exposes heavy rock cover is good for poke polling. Try Salt Point or any of your favorite abalone spots. Lightly salted, peppered, and floured, eel chunks are incredible when fried in butter and olive oil.

Please, please, please, wear a wader belt while slopping through the kelp. Your neoprene waders may float, but hypothermia is only a dunk away. The good and the bad–you don't see too many people while you're out on the reefs during midwinter–but that means fewer people to pull your tail out of a tough spot. Fish with a buddy.

GEESE

After an imprudent night out, many years ago, and a pre-sunrise entry into a dark duck blind the next morning, I happened to doze off. I guess my dog was also feeling the effects of a late night because, just as the sun was rising, we were both blissfully snoring away.

All that bliss ended when ten thousand snow geese, more or less, simultaneously lifted off a rice field fifty yards away. To say that the dog and I elevated to consciousness would be this year's understatement winner. We were elevated out of our seats. By the time we finally fell back into our respective hiding places, we were surrounded by the said ten thousand geese, all screaming at the top of their goose lungs and beating their goose wings. The sound, and air impact of that many geese getting up at once, is much like being on top of a freight train, in a long tunnel. It was the stuff of nightmares . . . and dreams.

Needless to say, we harvested a number of the large, migratory birds.

I'm told that the passage of geese in California's Sacramento Valley, in the mid-nineteenth century, blotted out the sun. When most of the Sacramento Valley was veldt, populated by antelope, elk, and grizzly bears, the winter goose population was in the millions of birds.

By the early twentieth century, the goose populations in California plummeted owing, primarily, to overhunting. Today, the snow goose population, and other goose populations, have become so large as to jeopardize the species.

The development of large-scale agriculture in California, and throughout the snow goose's various migratory paths in the United States, has led to what wildlife managers consider to be approaching over-population. The problem with too many geese is that in the spring, when the geese begin their reverse migration, and head back to Canada and Alaska to mate and hatch their young, their numbers wreak havoc with the delicate northern tundra. Too many geese and too little to eat at the edge of the arctic is a bad combination for both the geese and their environment.

Goose bags in the U.S. have been increased, almost annually, by Federal and state game managers. In Texas, the limit is ten snow geese. That may increase. Historically, the California limit has been three snow geese. However, owing to the fact that the goose population, particularly the snow goose population, has increased dramatically over the past decade, the limits have been increased on all species of wild geese, including dark geese, the Canada geese, and their subspecies, as well as white-fronted geese known locally as "speckle belly geese" or "specs." You can take thirty geese per day and have ninety in your possession!

Snow geese are the primary goose quarry in California. There are large populations of Canada geese, "honkers," in the valley and, usually, large flocks of white-fronted geese. But the numbers of dark geese are far surpassed by the huge flocks of snow geese.

Geese begin to arrive in the Sacramento Valley in late September, the specs usually arriving first. Once the big flocks settle in, usually by November, they spend their nights in the various game refuges that are managed throughout the Sacramento and Central Valley by the Federal Fish and Wildlife Service.

Typically, after the sun rises, the geese leave the refuges in smaller flocks of five to one hundred geese and head out to surrounding rice fields where they meet up with thousands of their brethren in what are known as "grinds." A goose grind, particularly a snow goose grind, is a spectacular sight. Thousands of bright white geese milling around, some with their heads down in the cut rice stalks, searching for loose rice grains, others, the sentinels, with their heads up, watching for danger. From a distance, it appears to have magically snowed on fields that rarely even suffer frost.

Hunting for geese in the valley is mainly done from blinds in ponds while duck hunting. Geese specialists, however, will target the goose proclivity for grinding in open, dry fields. To do this, goose hunters will dig pits in harvested fields to conceal themselves. Around the pits, they will spread massive numbers of decoys to imitate a goose grind in progress. The decoys can be as elaborate as precisely painted, plastic replicas of geese, or as simple as white rags tied to stakes, which flutter in the wind, to portions of cut-up tires painted black and spread across the field.

Added to concealment is the use of a goose call to, hopefully, draw the birds closer to your position, and the patience to wait until the large birds are within range, before you start shooting.

Geese produce large amounts of meat. Canadas and specs are traditionally roasted. Snows, however, don't lend themselves to roasting since, but for their breast, there is not much meat on a snow . . . and certainly no fat.

Snow goose breasts are great for frying or barbecuing. As with all wild game, **DO NOT OVERCOOK GOOSE BREASTS**! The prior note can be overlooked if you like tough, liver-tasting meat. Otherwise, less cooking is better.

My hunting partner, Ken Vignati, treats goose breasts like veal. He will make both scaloppini and stroganoff out of the breasts. To do this, you slice the breasts into quarter-inch to half-inch rounds, then salt, pepper, and lightly flour them. At this point, you sauté onions, garlic, and mushrooms. I sometimes like to add pre-cooked carrots or sweet peppers to the vegetables. When your vegetables are cooked, remove them from the heat and fire up some oil. I like olive oil, but peanut oil has a higher smoke point (you can get it hotter without it burning and smoking). Quick-fry the floured goose rounds until just lightly browned. This is usually enough time to adequately cook the goose (to coin a phrase).

Now you need to make a choice. For scaloppini, you pour out most of the oil you cooked the goose in and add some butter. When the butter's melted, scrape up any little bits of goose and fried flour from the bottom of the pan and add some more flour. When the flour has absorbed the butter, and browned a little bit, add some broth to make a gravy. Mix the vegetables, goose, and gravy and pour over rice, pasta, or polenta.

For stroganoff, you mix the vegetables and goose with sour cream and serve as above.

My partner also uses the goose legs and thighs, which have some meat. He saves up several dozen legs and thighs, boils them in a court-bouillon until nearly done, drains them, flours them, and then quick fries them in hot oil.

My favorite use for goose breasts is in sausage.

HALIBUT

Threadold story goes, "How do you tell a halibut from a flounder? You stick your finger in the fish's mouth . . . and if your finger comes back . . . it's a flounder."

Besides salmon, lingcod, and rockfish, the waters off the Sonoma coast provide excellent fishing for halibut up to twenty pounds.

Two species of halibut populate our coastal waters. The California halibut, which is the smaller of the two species, and the Pacific halibut, which will grow into multi-hundred pound bruisers. Catching a Pacific halibut is a rarity as most of the halibut south of Fort Bragg are California halibut.

Halibut are interesting creatures. When they are born they look like most other fish. They swim upright and have an eye on each side of their head.

Early in life, young halibuts get strange. They begin to lean over, usually to the right, and swim on their right side, near the bottom. Pretty soon, their right eye begins a journey from the right side of their head, to join the other eye on the left side of their head.

Eventually, the fish lives on its right side permanently. A minority of halibut end up with both eyes on the right side.

Halibut are aggressive and fierce feeders. They have long sharp teeth and are incredibly strong. Halibut lay buried in sandy bottoms, with only their eyes showing, looking up for smaller fish to pass over them. Their flat form gives them amazing leverage which creates the awesome swimming speed they use to explode up out of the sand to attack food fish.

In July, the halibut enter the shallow waters off our coast to spawn. Bodega Bay, including both the inner and outer bays, are great places to fish for halibut. Many people fish for them from the jetties at the mouth of Bodega Bay.

Tomales Bay is probably the prime halibut fishery in Northern California. Tomales has miles of shallow, sandy bottom and huge schools of anchovies, herring, and sardines during the summer. The halibut move into Tomales Bay to mate and gorge on the bait fish that are driven into the bay by the tides. (So do the white sharks . . . but that's another story.)

South of Tomales, Ten Mile Beach, which ends at Point Reyes, is another halibut factory. During July and August, it isn't unusual to end up catching both king salmon and halibut on the same trip off Ten Mile.

There are lots of ways to catch halibut. Fishing with live bait is probably the most effective. Unfortunately, nobody currently sells live bait at Bodega Bay. Most guys make their own bait using a "Sabiki" rig, which is a leader strung with multiple small flies and fished with a very light rod. This rig will catch jacksmelt, herring, and shiner perch. All three baits will catch halibut but the herring and jacksmelt are the better baits.

You can also net your own bait with a cast net. Most mornings during July and August, you can see guys throwing cast nets off the bow of their boats into the flats in Bodega Bay, making bait for halibut fishing. However you obtain the bait, you will need a live bait container to keep them alive. A live bait keeper can be as elaborate as a built-in tank with recirculating seawater, or as simple as a five-gallon bucket with an aerator hooked to your boat's batteries.

If you can't get live bait, you can use frozen anchovies or herring.

Live bait is usually drift-fished. The typical rig has a circle hook on an eighteen-inch leader that is attached to a three-way swivel. A drop weight, of sufficient size to keep the rig on the bottom while you drift in the current, is attached to the swivel with a six-inch leader. The swivel is then attached to your fishing line. The bait fish is hooked through its lips.

This rig is usually left to drag across the bottom as you drift with the current or wind. From a jetty, the rig is rigged with enough weight to keep it in one place while the live bait swims around.

The weight has a secondary function besides keeping the rig on the bottom. As you drift, the weight will kick up sand from the bottom, which will also attract halibut, or wake them up if you drag it across their heads.

Rather than drifting, you can troll for halibut. This can be done with live bait but usually involves slowly trolling large salmon lures, like Krocodiles or silver Apex's behind a flasher, or two, and a pound, or two, of lead weight.

Finally, spearfishing for halibut is great fun. The typical setup in these parts is to have one diver in the water, on scuba, who holds on to a water ski tow rope, while his buddy steers the boat. As the diver is pulled along, he focuses all his attention on the sandy bottom (which is usually very close to his face as the water visibility in Tomales Bay is usually no more than a couple of feet). When you see a halibut's eyes, and that's usually all you can see, you fire your spear just behind the eyes.

The only problem with this method is that Tomales Bay is the cornerstone of the "Red Triangle," where 90 percent of all white shark attacks occur, and where the whites return each summer to breed.

Viewed from afar, the practice of halibut spearing from a tow rope looks remarkably like trolling for a white shark with your buddy as bait. My wife discouraged the practice.

Maybe the hardest part of catching halibut is cooking them. It is really easy to ruin halibut. After you have cleaned and skinned the fish, you can cut it into steaks or fillets. Coat the pieces in olive oil and give them a good crust of salt, pepper, garlic powder, and maybe some dry Italian herbs. Barbeque the fish in a fish basket for less than six minutes to the inch. The difference between overcooked halibut and perfectly rare halibut is an overcooked fast food burger to a perfectly cooked fillet steak. Always err on the side of less cooking.

JERKY

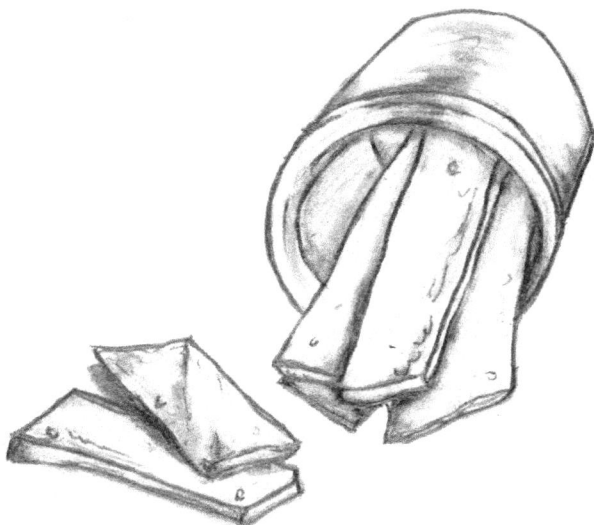

The brown, dried-out rectangle of what was once venison that my hunting buddy handed me didn't look much like breakfast. In fact, it looked like something the dog rejected (or had previously consumed).

But I trusted the guy, so I took a tentative bite. All of a sudden, my mouth exploded in a galaxy of flavor. There was sweet, sour, hot, spicy, and nourishment . . . all at once.

This was no ordinary jerky. This was manna, a gift from above.

In its simplest form, jerky is nothing more than dried meat left in the dryer longer than smoked meat. It is more durable and long-lasting than smoked meat because it has virtually all the moisture naturally found in animal flesh, as well as virtually all the brine added to the meat to cure it, removed in the drying process.

The native Pomo jerked both deer and salmon. Jerked meat could keep in a basket most of the summer and fall, or at least until the first salmon moved up into the river.

Making jerky involves much the same process as smoking meat. For a deer, most hunters save the scrap meat that is left over after the deer has been boned. I've known a hunter or two who will jerk out an entire deer.

Different parts of the deer are usually reserved for jerky if the hunter wants to use more than just scrap meat. Shoulders, hocks, and flanks work well for jerky. The secret to using these cuts is to slice the meat across the grain whenever you can. This will leave the final product slightly less tough. Try to cut the scraps into pieces no thicker than a quarter-inch.

The flank, which is the most popular part for jerking, can't really be cut across the grain, so it is usually used as it comes off the deer.

The meat can then be marinated in a salt brine. Two-thirds sugar to one-third salt works pretty well.

After the meat air dries, sprinkle it with garlic powder, black pepper, and, if you need that extra punch in your snacking, red pepper flakes. The meat then goes into the dryer.

The inexpensive dryers you can buy at hardware stores work great for jerky as well as for drying fruits and vegetables. You put the meat in the dryer, turn it on, and let it run until the meat reaches the desired level of dryness.

When it's done, the meat should be bendable without cracking. If it cracks, it will still be okay, but just a little harder to chew.

I've had jerked deer, moose, antelope, caribou, elk, duck, goose, turkey, salmon, trout, and bear. It's all good. But the recipe for the best jerky I've ever had was taught to me by Bob Sciaini.

Bob takes un-marinated scrap deer meat in chunks and runs it through a food processor to make a course mush. This avoids most of the "cutting across the grain" hassle. Here's where Bob and I part company. Rather than grinding up the meat scraps as they are, I marinate the chunks in that most superior of all marinades–Kikkoman Teriyaki Marinade . . . nothing else. I know that sounds tacky, but Kikkoman is a fabulous mix of salty soy and sugar, and it's so darned easy to just pour a bottle of it over the meat and walk away.

I let the meat soak a day or so, and then I return to Bob's recipe. I drain the meat and grind it in a food processor. The resulting mush gets put in a bread tin and placed in the freezer. After an hour or so, give or take, the mush is partially frozen. At this point, you turn the loaf of mush out on a cutting board and slice perfectly shaped rectangles of quarter-inch-thick marinated venison.

This product goes into my smoker where it is slowly dried to the proper consistency (bend but not break). The resulting jerky does not take leonine jaws to bite off a chunk, holds a world of flavor, and keeps just as long as traditionally jerked meat.

KIDS

GREAT WHITE SHARK

I read somewhere, probably in Jim Freeman's old outdoor column in the *San Francisco Chronicle Sporting Green* (when it was green), that kids who pick up fishing while they are young are rarely the kids who get into trouble when they are teenagers.

In my experience, that note of wisdom seems to hold pretty true.

I'm not sure why that is the case. Maybe it's the confidence a kid feels when he or she believes, for the first time, that they are competent to do something adult . . . as though putting a worm on a hook is adult.

Maybe it's when a kid senses that he or she is stepping outside of his or her little world, and is making their presence known in a different universe.

Or maybe it's just an adrenalin junkie's first hit. There's a living thing at the end of the line that's probably madder than hell at them, but whose capture is, at that moment, the only important thing in the world to them.

Or maybe it's just that first tingling of the instinct to survive and to provide for the tribe.

Geeze, it's just fun . . . and kids appreciate fun.

Nonetheless, I love teaching kids to fish. In most cases, once a kid has landed a fish and seen the results of the technique and technology–hooks and worms–it's not hard to keep them interested, at least for a while.

My dad got me hooked on fishing at Lake Merced, in San Francisco. He would get off the train from work in the City, grab a sandwich, and we, my sisters included, would head to the lake, rent a boat, and spend foggy, windy, summer evenings catching planter rainbow trout.

My dad taught all my cousins to fish with single salmon eggs drifted past boulders on the south fork of the Eel River. They all still love to fish.

Fall is one of the best times to introduce a kid to fishing. Of course, you can always take a kid to a trout farm and, for a healthy per pound price, let a kid reel in a first fish. But in fall, there are plenty of wild fish to chase in kid fashion.

We are very lucky here in Cloverdale since we have Lake Sonoma, Lake Mendocino, and the Russian River so accessible.

In September, right through until it starts to turn cold, angling for panfish in Lake Sonoma is about as kid-friendly as it gets. It helps to have a boat, but you don't need one. There are plenty of trails around the lake that can get you into some of the brushy canyon coves that ring the lake. If you've got a boat, it's just easier to get to the coves.

Starting in about September, the red-eared sunfish, Sacramento perch, crappie, and bluegill start to feed higher in the water column. With winter on its way, these fish try to load up on the last of the flying insects that make up such a large portion of their protein intake. Right when they are feeling like gorging themselves is the best time to introduce them to a kid.

Panfish, when you find them, are pretty easy to catch . . . that's why they are good kid targets. Most kids will give fishing an honest chance to entertain them. But you are just not going to find an eight-year-old who is going to sit patiently with a promise of a trophy fish. Kids need fairly quick and consistent results.

A typical rig for panfish is a small, size twelve or fourteen hook, tied on above a lightweight, a large split shot is enough, with a bobber attached above the hook. The bobber should be about eighteen to twenty-four inches above the hook, depending on the cover and sunlight. You should be able to buy the whole rig, rod, reel, and tackle, for less than twenty dollars. Red worms make great bait, as do mealworms and crappie jigs . . . weighted flies.

Look for open areas that are adjacent to flooded brush or trees. The panfish will hang in the water at the edge of the brush waiting for targets of opportunity. There is nothing that will open a kid's eyes wider than a dinner plate than a bobber suddenly disappearing under the water as a fish has taken the bait.

When I was a kid, there was no such thing as catch-and-release. We ate everything we caught. In fact, that was the rule, you catch it . . . you eat it. My kids were brought up on the same mantra.

Since then, and in the face of threatened species all over the planet, catch-and-release fishing has become an important, and responsible, part of the sport.

I think it is probably a good idea to instill catch-and-release in kids. In the future, considering the plight of many species of fish, it may be the only fishing left.

Releasing fish is actually pretty easy with kids. First, most kids love to see caught fish taken off the hook and permitted to swim away. It's more like a cartoon that way than an exercise in survival. And . . . well . . . kids don't like to eat fish anyway.

If you do keep the fish, their tiny fillets are great dredged in flour and quick fried in butter and olive oil. For a treat even the kids will like, soak the fillets for a day or two in a very sugar-heavy brine, with some salt and a little soy sauce for flavor, and then smoke them for six hours. The fillets come out like candy. Great snacks.

LIMPETS
AND TURBAN
SNAILS

"It tastes like garlic," she said.

"It's supposed to taste like garlic," I said. "It's French. But what about those little meaty jobs? What do they taste like?" I asked.

"Oh they taste fine . . . but, they taste like garlic."

My wife's sole flaw, after twenty-five years of marriage, is that she does not like garlic.

The meaty little jobs that she found garlicky were limpets and turban snails . . . my latest foray into the tide pool world.

On a recent abalone dive arranged by my realtor friends, Jane and Ron Pavelka, I got tired of getting bashed into wash rocks by steady sets of three-foot surf, so I decided to settle for medium size abs and save my oversized body for a later trip.

As I made my ungainly crawl back through the boulder field that was exposed by the minus tide, I noticed lots and lots of limpets and turban snails attached to the rocks. I knew that they were edible, and a staple of the Coast Miwoks and Pomos, but I had never taken the time away from an abalone harvest to take much notice of them.

This time, I was grateful for any diversion that would get me out of the rough water and delay the long climb up the cliff and back to the car. I started prying the little buggers off with my abalone iron and soon had a nice double handful of gastropod mollusks.

Limpets are much like small abalones. They are in the same family of mollusks as abalone and are designed like an abalone. Limpets have a single shell that protects a muscular foot with which they attach themselves to underwater rocks. Limpets creep across wash rocks feeding on algae.

A good size limpet is about the size of a quarter, but they range up to a couple of inches across. They are often referred to as "Chinese hats" owing to the fact that they are shaped like a flattened cone with a tiny peak. Needless to say, it takes quite a few limpets to make a meal.

Turban snails look like nothing more than slightly iridescent garden snails. They are rather small, about half the size of a ping-pong ball. Turban snails are also mollusks and behave much the same as abalone and limpets. They also cruise along the rocks that are either underwater or periodically covered by wave action. The snails also have a single shell and live on algae.

The fact that both limpets and turban snails live on algae makes them a very important part of the tidal environment. They are the groundskeepers of the tide pools, making sure all the algae is neatly trimmed.

Perhaps more importantly to humans is that the gastropods are algae eaters, and not filter feeders, like clams, oysters, and mussels. As filter feeders, clams, oysters, and mussels let seawater pass through their filtering systems and draw nutrients out of the water. Unfortunately, during the summer months (any month without an "r" in it as the old adage goes), the filter feeders consume toxic micro-organisms along with the other food they strain out of seawater. These micro-organisms, the same critters that create "red tides," can kill you (or at least put you off shellfish for the rest of your life). The limpets and turban snails don't live on microorganisms; they're vegetarians, so you can eat them all year.

The harvest of limpets and turban snails is regulated by the Fish and Game regulations covering invertebrates. You may take a combination of thirty-five snails and/or limpets. That's about a meal for one person. You can't harvest limpets or snails in state parks or state reserves.

The garlic, to which my wife took exception, was on the gastropods because cooking snails in garlic and parsley, à la French escargot, is about the only way I know how to prepare them.

I made this up, so there is probably a better recipe out there somewhere. I put about an inch of half water, half white wine into a saucepan and brought it to a boil. I threw the limpets and snails in the boiling liquid for three minutes, per my egg timer, and then plunged them into cold water. After a minute or two, I drained the collection. By and large, the limpets had separated themselves from their shells and sat in the strainer as little morsels of meat about the size of the end of my little finger.

The snails were another story. These I treated like their French cousins and twisted-pulled the meat out with a nut pick. It came out very easily as soon as I got the move down. It's kind of a twisting/pinching maneuver that's all in the wrist. There was a little shell-like piece attached to the end of the snail's foot, which it uses to seal itself in its shell. These come off easily.

While I was tending to the snails, I had a handful of parsley, chopped fine with a couple of cloves of garlic, sauteing gently in olive oil. I added the snails and limpets to the mix for about a minute, added salt and pepper, and voila, snails and limpets a la Francois.

I noted on a website that the limpets will substitute for clams in about any recipe for linguine or chowder. The snails are, well, just snails.

LINGCOD

B eing, as I am, in my other life, a trial lawyer, I'm in regular contact with predators of all sizes and dispositions. But, frankly, I've never run into a lawyer or judge who could match a lingcod for sheer cussedness or dogged orneriness.

Lingcod are one of the truly great treasures of the Pacific coast. Off the Sonoma coast, lingcod will grow to more than thirty pounds. They reside in and around rocky reefs. Lingcod especially enjoy caves where they can hide the bulk of their bodies while waiting for dinner to swim past their camouflaged face.

And what a face it is. Next to the horrific mug of the cabezone, the first ugliest fish off the coast, the lingcod comes in a very close second. First, the head is enormous, with a wide, gaping mouth full of long sharp teeth. The eyes bulge and the nostrils appear to flare. Lingcod always look mad.

Mostly, a lingcod is an eating machine. It is almost always an amazing experiment to open the stomach of a boated lingcod. You are almost always assured to find a cross-section of sea dwellers in the ling. I've found fish nearly as long as the lingcod that ate them. I've found huge crabs, abalone, clams, enormous octopus, squid, rocks, lures, beer cans, and plastic things I could not identify.

Lingcod fishing is good most of the year but only legal from July (or as set by the DF&W) to the end of the year. It is especially good toward September when the larger fish come into shallow waters to spawn. During the season, you can catch lings in water from 20 feet to 300 feet. Current fishing regulations, however, limit fishing to waters of less than 180 feet (or as set by the DF&W). This has been the rule for several years now. It is an attempt to permit several species of rockfish, which have seen their populations shrink, to build up their stock.

Lingcod were more severely regulated a couple of years ago when it was thought that they were being overfished. After a year of requiring that lingcod must be thirty inches long to be legal, and making the limit one fish, the scientific types decided that the population wasn't as damaged as was believed. The length limit has been returned to twenty-four inches and you can keep two fish.

Lingcod are usually caught by jigging weighted lures. Jigging means lowering the lure quickly until it hits bottom, then reeling it back to the surface in a jerking fashion. Most lingcod seem to hit the jig just as the lure hits the bottom. In most cases, the bottom is a boulder or ledge associated with a reef.

While it has become popular to fish the inshore reefs for rockfish using freshwater bass equipment, lightweight rods, reels, and line, going light would be folly when attempting to land a lingcod.

It only takes having a couple of lings hit your jig to be able to tell immediately that you have hooked a lingcod and not just a large rockfish. These fish are brutes. When hooked, their first inclination is to head for a cave and pull you in with them. They have an uncanny ability to wrap fishing line around any available rock and make it impossible for you to reel them into the boat.

The really fun part about lingcod fishing is that most of the lingcod that get up to the boat, but not necessarily into the boat, come up as "hitchhikers." The typical ling episode involves lowering your jig in free-spool, which means with no reel pressure on the line, having the jig hit the rocky bottom beneath the boat, beginning to reel the jig back to the boat, and then feeling the light to moderate jerking of a rockfish that has attacked your jig and become hooked. *Okay,* you think, *I'll just reel this nice little rockfish up and add him to the bag.*

About three cranks of the reel later the little rockfish stops and heads back to the bottom, notwithstanding the fact that you are trying to pull him to the surface with everything you've got. When you are finally able to muscle that little rockfish to the surface, you realize that he is surrounded by the head of a huge lingcod, which is attached to the enormous body of a very mad lingcod.

A landing net is your best friend at this point as the lingcod is probably six or seven times larger than the rockfish that it is still trying to swallow. Big lings are amazingly tenacious. I've landed them in the boat, and while on the deck, they are still trying to gulp down the other fish.

Lingcod are apparently fearless. I've pulled big lings to the surface and landed them, and clamped to their flanks was another bigger lingcod. I've pulled many big lingcod into the boat who bore lacerations along their entire body from some other, even bigger ling, who was trying to swallow them while I was reeling them in. I mean, it is an attitude thing with lings.

After their aggressiveness, and mean looks, the next thing that shocks folks new to lingcod fishing is the color of lingcod meat. Simply said . . . it's green. Well, actually it ranges from a pale Nile green to a brilliant turquoise. But, in the end, it's green. There is a slightly different species, the kelp greenling, which also has green meat, but these are not lingcod.

However, fear not, intrepid cook. When put to heat, the lingcod's meat turns a creamy white. And what meat it is: flaky, firm, and moist. Lingcod is one of those fish that will stand up to just about any kind of cooking. You can barbeque it, batter and deep fry it, sauté it, bake it, or eat it raw. It's a very safe fish because you can make a mistake with too much heat and not ruin it like a halibut or tuna.

My current favorite recipe comes from the Sonoma Diet, by Connie Guttersen. You lay out some parchment paper, about twenty inches off the roll, and fold it in half. Open the folded paper and arrange some chopped fresh (or canned if it's wintertime), tomatoes, and some chopped fennel root on one half of the paper. Drizzle the pile with olive oil in which you've lightly cooked some chopped garlic. Lightly salt and pepper the pile.

Then, add a pile of chopped, roasted sweet red peppers, some chopped, cured olives, and maybe some shredded zucchini or chopped green onion. Drizzle with more of the garlic olive oil. Lightly salt and pepper that layer. Put a piece of lingcod filet on the pile. Lightly salt and pepper the filet, drizzle it with garlic olive oil and a little lemon juice. Top the whole pile with grated lemon peel, and shredded basil leaves.

Fold the other half of the paper over the pile, roll the edges of the two paper halves together to seal the package, and twist the corners to keep it sealed. Cook the packages at 400 degrees for twelve to fifteen minutes. Lingcod en papillote. Awesome.

LOBSTERS

Three's foraging, and then there's foraging. This time of year foraging can be as simple as gathering feral plumbs, or as exotic as grabbing spiny lobsters. This is a lobster story.

Each year, in the first week of October, the lobster season opens. Catching lobster is always far more than just grabbing crustaceans; it is the full-body experience.

The lobster trip begins with a casual, late morning Wednesday drive south on Highway 5, to Ventura, with dive-buddy Mike. We arrive in Southern California with plenty of time to buy last-minute scuba attachments, always overpriced, and pick up Fish and Game "Ocean Enhancement" stamps for our fishing licenses.

After greeting old mates from past trips, we store our gear aboard the dive boat, "Spectre," our eighty-foot home for the next four days, and go ashore for a last meal on terra firma.

Spectre casts its lines at 9:00 p.m. and heads south at a comfortable fifteen knots. It's always a little strange getting used to a berth on a dive boat. They are very narrow, short, and do not permit you to quite sit up. Add to that the rumble of the diesel motors, and the rock of an eleven-foot sea swell, and it usually results in less than a full first night's sleep.

Around 6:30 a.m., Captain Ted, who has shared all-night driving duties with the crew, pulls back on the throttles, and you can feel the human electricity surge through the boat. A climb up the companionway to the main deck reveals excited divers donning wet suits, the smell of bacon from the galley, and nothing but ocean to the horizon.

This year's excursion was to the Cortez Bank, a 110-mile boat ride south from Ventura, and about the same distance west of San Diego. The Cortez Bank is the top of an undersea mountain that rises from a seabed a mile deep, to about twenty-five feet from the surface. The diveable surface is about three-quarters of a mile by two-and-a-half miles and ranges from twenty-five feet deep to the drop-off at about one-hundred feet deep. The bank supports a giant kelp forest which supports a wildlife population so concentrated as to rival any aquarium you may visit.

After a final check of your scuba equipment, and the myriad attachments to your buoyancy compensator and weight belt including net bag, dive computer, compass, knife, measuring tool, emergency whistle, dive light (and spare), pole spear, ab iron (for scallops), and extra things you may not remember why you brought, you jump off the eight-foot-high deck into the first dive of the year.

The stated point of lobster diving is to gather lobster, which must be done by hand. The most effective technique is to swim about six feet above the reef shining your diving light around the edges of rock piles, caves, and ledges. After several years of this, you learn to recognize the tips of lobster antennae by their reddish color, which only becomes apparent when the light from your lamp hits them (red coloration is filtered out under about thirty feet of seawater).

At this point, the fact that you have a buddy becomes apparent. Lobster diving is definitely a team sport. Generally, when you see the lobster antennae, it means that the rest of the bug is back in a hole. Now, most lobster holes have a back door for escape purposes. Stupid lobsters don't maintain back doors and end up in game bags pretty quick. After many years of this poking around, dive-buddy Mike and I are pretty much in tune with the hand signals and full-body gesticulations that indicate that one of us has found a lobster and that the other should go find the back door and park himself there.

About the only way you can safely catch a lobster is to sneak your hand up on him while he's watching you and grab a substantial part of him. Grabbing an antenna or single leg is rarely successful as they break off fairly easily when a bug is trying to get away from your hold. Generally, you have to go back into the cave in which the bug is living and get close enough to grab down on his body and hold him down until you get a good grip on his carapace (the front shell). Sometimes, you can get your hands on a couple of legs and work your way up to the body.

Once you get a hold of a bug, the battle is only half over. Lobsters are *very* strong for their size and *very* fast swimmers. Their main means of quick locomotion is a tail scoop, which propels them backwards like a rocket. But when they want to walk backwards, like when you may have grabbed a leg or two or a couple of antennae, they can nearly pull you into a cave.

If you're lucky, and get a good hold, you pull the bug out, hold him tight to your chest while measuring him for legal size, and then put him in the bag. Half the time the bug tries to escape through the back door. Hopefully, your dive-buddy is on the ball and can snag the critter on his way out.

You get to keep seven lobster a day. I've never caught that many, although Mike and I did catch a nine-pound lobster a couple of years ago during a night dive off San Nicholas Island.

As I said, the stated reason for the trip is to catch lobster. The real reason to go is to spend four days at sea, with good friends, a good crew, and a good ship's cook amidst an environment unlike any other. Usually, there are about fifteen daylight dives and four night dives.

Diving the offshore seamounts is like no other foraging. For four days of diving, you never see any evidence of humanity whatsoever. It is the fish's world and we just get a chance to swim through it. The night dives are especially otherworldly as all you see are the sleeping fish and sharks in the narrow beam of your light. Out in the inkiness, beyond the lamp glow, creatures large and small leave phosphorescent trails as they dash away like meteorites in space.

MANZANITA

Several years ago, I found myself on my hands and knees dragging my old 30-30 deer rifle inside a leafy tunnel that ran through an enormous stand of manzanita. Theoretically, I was deer hunting—mostly, I was trying to stay alive by avoiding having to traverse a shale slide that was incredibly steep, anything but stable, and which ended 200 feet below in an escape-proof granite draw.

None of this bothered me as much as the distinct smell, all around me, of wild pigs. The tunnel I was in was a pig freeway running along the slope, and the way I saw it, I was at about eye level with a decent-sized boar's tusks. That's when I decided I hated manzanita.

But, as they say, I've seen the light. Manzanita is incredible!

Manzanita is the ubiquitous shrub we see on the hills all around Cloverdale. It has smooth red bark with twisting branches and round leaves. It hugs the ground but can grow to over fifteen feet tall. The Spanish translation for manzanita is "little apple," which aptly describes the appearance of the manzanita fruit.

Native Californians up and down the coast harvested manzanita for an incredible variety of uses, using nearly every part of the bush.

Kids would eat the flowers for a treat. These were collected in the late winter and early spring. In July and August, the women would take their children out to harvest manzanita berries. The women would beat the bushes with sticks, letting the berries fall into woven baskets. These berries were the real treasure.

Manzanita cider was, before the European invasion, the universal California drink. The ripe berries were dried in the sun and then crushed or roughly broken. The resulting mash was soaked in water until the berry essence was leached out and then filtered in woven sieves. Sometimes, fresh berries were used for the cider but the preferred method was to dry the berries first.

The resulting cider would keep for several days. I have not read where the Pomo ever let the cider ferment but I can't help but believe that this didn't occur from time to time.

Besides drinking the manzanita cider, the Pomo cooks would make a fine mash or flour-like substance from dried berries. This mash was a staple when baked into cookies and breads. The mash could be stored for use during the hard times in winter.

The Pomo mixed the berry mash with salmon eggs to make a high-protein, high-carbohydrate loaf that, after baking, would keep long enough to provide food for a long hunt or trek to the coast for abalone and seaweed. During the early summer, the mash could be mixed with dried wild plums and baked or dried.

The berry mash was also boiled using very hot rocks in a waterproof basket to make a mush. Berries would be added to the mush making for a real treat.

The Pomo made tea out of the manzanita bark. It was said to ease nausea and upset stomach.

Manzanita makes great firewood for outdoor cooking. Once it has burned to coals, it will produce high heat for an extended period.

The best poison oak remedy I have ever used is easy to make and readily available to Cloverdale residents. Manzanita grows all around us and is easily harvested. Take a shopping bag full of manzanita leaves and cover them with water in a large pot. Boil the leaves for a half-hour or so until they have broken down and become somewhat mushy. Strain the leaves out of the resulting tea and store it in the refrigerator.

The resulting liquid is a very strong astringent which, if you generously apply to poison oak irritation, will quickly dry the weeping, and provide phenomenal itch relief.

MUSHROOMS

B eginning with the first rains in October, and running through mid-spring, the North Coast explodes in a hidden forest of fungus. It's mushroom time.

When steelhead fishing is nixed because the rivers are so thick with mud you can walk across them it's time for a walk in the woods.

Mushroom hunting is probably the least equipment intensive, and most calming forager pursuit. It is, in fact, a walk in the woods. You can take your dog without fear that it will chase off the game. You can take your kids and wear them out a little. You can even take your wife and actually enjoy some peace and quiet together.

Mushrooming is best enjoyed on a drippy overcast day when the wind is down. That combination seems to sharpen the soft silence of the deep woods and helps to heighten your visual senses.

It's the eyes you need for finding fungus. You can't call them, and unless you're a trained dog, you can't sniff them out. They do not leap or flush to expose themselves. You just have to look for them.

The nice thing is that mushrooms don't run away. In fact the same species will likely be seen sprouting in the same spot year after year. That is why the old Italians won't tell you where they got their last batch of big reds or coccoras.

Most mushrooms are found off the trail which means you must be aware of the fact that poison oak does not simply go away in the winter. Even if you can't see those festive red leaves of fall, there is enough blister raising oil in denuded poison oak branches to make you wish you'd never left the big city.

Find a forested area where you can walk around casually, poking here and there. The coastal parks are great places to gather but be aware of the rules about where, when and how much you can take. It varies.

After a while of staring at the forest floor you start seeing things you would have missed if you were just walking through. Your eyes sharpen, and your vision widens. Just the hint of a fungus under a leaf will catch the attention you would ordinarily pay to eye level objects. It doesn't take long to get into the zone.

Use your light weight foraging stick, your number 9 or 10, to gently move the forest detritus from on top of the mushrooms to get a better look. Please don't go rooting through the forest floor like a hungry hog after an acorn, we've got lots of those already. You can seriously damage the underground organism, called the mycelium that is responsible for the exposed mushroom.

Typically, around here, the first mushrooms to show are the coccora. They will be up around ten days after the first good October rain. Generally next up are the French reds and Italian reds. Those are the boletes which are especially favored by locals because they eat and dry so well.

A little later in the season, when the temperatures start dropping for winter, the chanterelles begin to make their appearance. These, along with the matsutake may be the most prized fungus in our neighborhood.

Pinkies show up on sloping grassy fields and are a favorite pickling fungus.

You will note that I have not described any of the mushrooms I have referred to. Nothing I write here will make mushroom hunting safe. That is because there are many mushrooms out there that will, at a minimum, make you sick if you eat them and, in some cases, will take your life with just a tiny bite. Several varieties of amanita, which look an awful lot like some perfectly delicious mushrooms, will make your liver look like old hamburger and likely result in your departure from the ranks of foragers.

The Old Italians, back again, use to go out on the grassy hills around South City and pick mushrooms around the cow pies. Then they'd drop them in boiling water with a penny. If the penny tarnished, the mushrooms were poisonous. Friends, please . . . do not try to gauge mushrooms in this manner. It's a wonder there were any "old" Italians at all.

Only . . . only . . . pick mushrooms with someone who is highly trained in the pursuit. It helps if they are still alive . . . it lends some credibility to their expertise. There are mushroom groups throughout the county who will gladly take you along and walk you through the woods.

There are a number of excellent books on the subject. David Arora's "All That The Rain Promises" is great as is his "Mushrooms Demystified". But please remember, the best book is no assurance that what you are picking may not be your last meal.

My comments are in no way intended to dissuade anyone from chasing mushrooms. I love it and highly recommend it. Just do it right.

MUSSELS

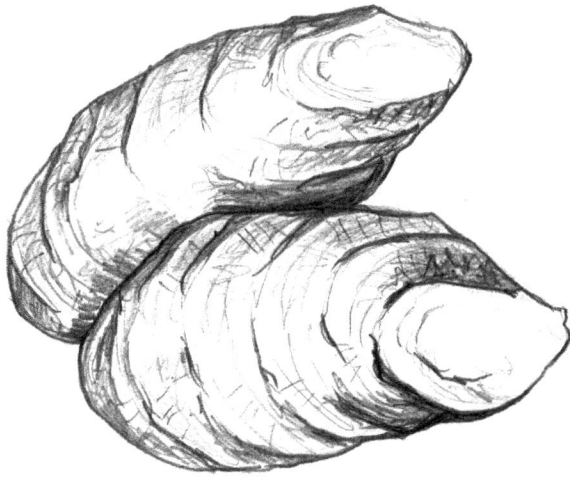

n some respects, being a pre-Spanish Pomo had to be a great gig. I mean, discounting the fact that you had to spend drippy winters in a woven willow hut, there were boundless sources of food available to you.

Some of the food took some work to obtain, killing deer for instance, or digging up wild lily bulbs. God did, however, apparently have a soft spot for lazy guys like me when he designed Sonoma County.

Take, for instance, mussels.

Mussels don't run or fly. They don't require digging or careful, time-consuming preparation (think acorns).

During the spring minus tides, the Pomos would travel to the coast to gather seaweed, pick abalone, dig clams, and harvest mussels. The seafood provided needed iodine, which was otherwise in short supply in a diet of acorns, venison, and berries.

Mussels live in the oceans and in estuaries, on rocks, and on man-made structures that are exposed at low tides. They are filter feeders who take their nourishment from the sea water that flows around them when they are submerged. Each individual mussel is attached to the rock or other surface by a mass of tough, hairy fibers called a byssus. They tend to live in colonies, so once you find one, you will probably find as many as you want.

Basically, you walk up to a mass of mussels and pull them off the rock. That's it . . . really! Sometimes, the byssus is pretty tough, so a knife or other tool makes removal a little easier.

Salt Point State Park is a great place to harvest mussels. There are lots of accessible rocks and other structures at low tides, but I have harvested mussels all along the coast.

The one thing you have to remember is that because mussels are filter feeders, during the summer, they will fill up on certain microorganisms that are pretty toxic. These are the same microorganisms that create red tides. As a result, California imposes a quarantine, and harvesting mussels is not permitted from May through October. During the winter months, they are safe to eat.

There is a little trick here, though. Take the little ones! California mussels can grow up to nine or ten inches long. Mussels are very flavorful. That flavor, however, grows more intense and much stronger as they get older. The large ones are just too strong to enjoy.

I learned this the hard way when a buddy and I decided that the best-all-time Superbowl snack was mussels. And since we were pretty young, and pretty impressed with size at the time, we gathered a bucket of the biggest mothers-of-all-mussels to serve to our friends. These suckers were as big as our hands. Very impressive!

After much preparation, and with a grand presentation, we proudly served our catch, only to watch our friends discretely lose the mussels into potted plants, ashtrays, napkins, and other disposal units.

Cooking mussels is as stupidly easy as harvesting them. While you can remove them from their shell, after steaming them open, and use them in spaghetti gravy, fritters, stews, or soups, my favorite is the easiest.

Treat the mussels like clams. In a large frying pan, sauté course chopped garlic, shallots, and parsley until tender. Add salt, pepper, and red pepper flakes. Cover the vegetables with white wine, and let it simmer a little while.

While all this is happening, have a friend clean the mussels. All this entails is scrubbing them lightly and trimming off their beards (the byssus).

Put the mussels into the pan and cover. Let them steam for five or six minutes and check to see if their shells have opened. Dump the ones that don't open as they were probably dead and not likely to taste good.

Pour the whole mess into a bowl so that the mussels will get some of the gravy inside their shells. Then just go to town opening the little buggers, pulling the meat out, and chowing down.

Of course, as with clams, etc., it is required that you are armed with a glass of wine and a loaf of French bread to soak up the mussel gravy.

OLIVES

"**Y**ou're trying to kill me for the insurance!"

"I'm not!"

"You want me to eat olives that you picked! Everybody knows that those things can kill you!"

"Well . . . maybe." (The pregnant pause, for effect, is a bad habit . . . I've got to quit that.)

Although they are not native to northern Sonoma County, olive trees are so common in our community as to be virtual natives. Olives are simply delicious and a major annual event in the forager's year.

October is the month in which local olives generally ripen. Even though they remain semi-green, most local varieties are ready to cure by the end of the month.

The best time to pick an olive is when it is about one-third purplish-reddish and the balance green. Generally, this is when the acid and oil in the olive are balanced. After being cured, these olives will turn fully green.

Picking olives is a touchy business. You can't just grab them and throw them in a bucket. I mean, you can, but you won't like the bruises you'll raise on the fruit. You see, olives are very sensitive. They're like anybody. If you treat them gently, you eventually get to the sweetness within.

I usually climb into an olive tree with a five-gallon plastic bucket, about one-quarter full of water, and then pick into it. This creates some cushioning and will prevent a lot of bruising. It doesn't however prevent being bruised when you fall out of a tree, so be careful! On the other hand, climbing trees is almost always fun and few of us get to do much of it.

There are some really great old olive trees in Cloverdale. Some have very large fruit and some have smaller fruit. The larger trees are probably the most efficient to pick, but sometimes the smaller fruit has a higher oil content. Oil content is very important in an olive because most of the flavor comes from the oil.

I don't know who the brave soul was who first ate a cured olive. If you put an uncured one in your mouth, you will immediately regret it and will remember the experience for a long time. Uncured olives are verrry bitter. The bitterness comes from the acid in the fruit.

Legend, and scientific hypothesis, has it that the first olives eaten came from a fruited branch that had bowed down into slowly moving brackish water. After sufficient time, the acid was leached out of the olives by the semi-salty water.

The forager does not have time to wait for nature to prep the hors d'oeuvres. Better living, and olives, through chemistry! If you want to neutralize an acid, the easiest way is to mix it with a base of sufficient strength. Out comes the Drano or Red Devil. These compounds are nothing more than pure lye, a nearly absolute base. (I know this is sounding weird, but stay with me.)

Once you get your prize fruits home, pick out the leaves and branches you may have added to the bucket and wash the olives. Again, throughout this whole process, you can bruise the olives by smacking them into one another. Be gentle.

Put the olives in a non-reactive container. This means don't use a metal container unless it is stainless steel. I have always used old clay or porcelain water cooler crocks that you can get at yard sales. Multi-gallon glass pickle jars work great too.

Fill the crock with cold water until the olives are covered by at least four inches of water. The lye solution formula is two ounces (about four level tablespoons) of lye to each gallon of water. Mix the lye with two quarts of cold water in a steel pot with a handle. Always add the lye to the water, not the other way around. You can hurt yourself if you do it the other way. Stir the water as you add the lye.

Then get to the crock as quickly as you can. Once you add lye to water, the lye starts to heat up and look for acid to neutralize. Don't spill this mixture on yourself as it might mistake you for an acid-based creature and try to neutralize you! At a minimum, the lye solution will burn you if it spills on you. Keep vinegar at hand to neutralize any lye that touches your skin.

Pour the lye solution over the olives and stir them a little with a wooden spoon. The olives won't cure unless they are emerged in the solution. If there are floaters, and there usually are, get a burlap sack, or a towel, and put it in the crock to push the olives down into the solution.

You are now done with the hard work. I usually pick olives after work and leave them in the solution overnight. In the morning, you take an olive out and wash it thoroughly. Then cut it in half to see if the lye has penetrated to the pit. You can see the change in color.

If the olive is still mostly bright green, as opposed to dull green, repeat the curing process with fresh lye. The second bath will usually only take half as long as the first. When the lye has completely permeated the olive, the olive's acid is neutralized. Don't over-cure the olives as it will make them mushy.

The next process is to gently wash the lye off the olives. This is nothing more than changing the water two or three times a day.

I usually only do it twice a day, morning and night. The old water cooler crocks are great for this as they have a hole at the bottom for the spout. You can plug this hole with a cork and just drain the olives from the bottom. Keep air away from the olives as best you can as it will discolor them.

The first time you drain the olives, the runoff will be a yellowish/ purplish/brownish color. Gradually, the color will change. When the olives drain clear, eat one. Really, it won't kill you!

What you do with the finished product is only limited by your imagination and some basic laws of biochemistry.

The easiest thing to do is to make a brine of four ounces of salt per gallon of water. If you refrigerate the olives in glass jars in this brine, they will keep for months (mine rarely last past the holidays as they are quickly consumed by my family and friends). To dress the olives, rinse the brine off them. I add a little olive oil, and a splash of vinegar, black pepper, crushed red pepper flakes, and French/Italian herbs (they are usually salty enough from the brine.)

Addressing my wife's concerns: The way people kill themselves with olives is when they try to can them. Don't try to can them. Botulism poisoning is a nasty way to die. If you try to use a hot water bath like your mother showed you, thinking that because the canning lid is sealed by a vacuum you are safe, you are dead, and I mean dead, wrong.

Botulism is caused by deadly spores that just love to multiply in anaerobic, near-vacuum, conditions. There are only two safe ways to can olives. You can use the high temperature created in a pressure canner (ten pounds of pressure for sixty minutes (basically ruins the olives anyway) or by hot water bath where the olives are in a high acid brine. Lemon juice or vinegar are typical acids used to create a high acid brine. My advice is to just refrigerate them, and eat them before, or during, the Super Bowl. (The best reference for canning olives is Division of Agricultural Sciences, University of California, Leaflet #2758.)

If you don't get to picking olives until December or January, and they have turned completely black on the tree, pack them in rock salt for a couple of months and try one. This is how the Greeks make their olives and they are very delicious.

PHEASANT

The concussive explosion of feathers from under my feet sent me straight up into the air, starting certain reactive mussels in my lower abdomen to pucker. My dog wasn't in much better shape, having only a second before he walked directly over nature's version of an IED.

By the time I'd pulled my shotgun up to my shoulder, and turned nearly 180 degrees, the big gaudy rooster pheasant was thirty yards away and employing evasive maneuvers.

My next mistake, one many hunters make on the opening day of pheasant season, was to shoot where the big bird had been, rather than where he was going. Needless to say, the first bird of the morning did not end up in my bag.

Pheasants are not indigenous to California. According to the non-profit group, Pheasants Forever, ". . . the pheasant, like many Americans, is an immigrant to North America." "The first successful introduction of pheasants to this country occurred in 1881 when Judge Owen Nickerson Denny (US consul to China) shipped 30 Chinese ringnecks (26 survived the journey) to his home in the Willamette Valley of Oregon. Eleven years later Oregon opened a 75-day season and hunters bagged 50,000 pheasants. They were subsequently released in 40 of the 50 states." Rooster pheasants are, far and away, the most colorful of our gamebirds.

Pheasants thrive in grasslands. I've shot at pheasants in southern Sonoma County, but our region does not sustain many pheasants. The big birds need plenty of grain and low cover to survive. The Sacramento Valley is ideal habitat for pheasants and serves as the primary destination for local pheasant hunters.

Because of modern farming techniques, which use every inch

of land available to raise crops, the population of wild pheasants is relatively small. Sixty years ago, farmers left wide swatches of land undisturbed because their equipment did not permit them to till, sew, or harvest as close to fence lines as modern equipment permits. Also, in those days, the pre-corporate farm days, farmers left more land aside for wildlife. They recognized the social and ecological value of having wild animals around their farms.

The effect of the new farming techniques is that, in order to provide pheasant hunting to the large number of individuals who find it to be the essence of hunting, wild birds are not relied on to provide a hunting population.

In the Willows area, where I and my friends hunt, there are several hunting clubs. The largest hunting clubs are run by service clubs, the Elks for instance, and churches. In Willows, both the Elks and the Catholic church have a long list of farmers who support them. These farmers give the clubs permission to hunt on their land. The clubs purchase pen-raised pheasants and then distribute them on the fields that have been donated.

Club members pay $125 to $150 to join the club and are then permitted to hunt all of the farmland that has been donated to the club.

The night before opening day, and on a couple of weekends after that, club members drive through the fields at night, dropping pheasants out of cages and onto the fields. The pheasants do what pheasants do, and immediately head for cover.

Most of the cover on these fields are long, weed-covered berms called "checks" that are used to control irrigation water in rice fields. In the morning hunters assemble and, at the stroke of 8:00 a.m., the hunt begins.

What attracts many, if not most pheasant hunters to the field, is watching the dogs. Dogs are to pheasant hunting as betting is to poker. You can still play, but it's nowhere near as interesting.

Highly trained field dogs will course in front of a line of hunters using their noses to tell them where a pheasant is or has been. Once a pheasant is located, hiding in the brush or tall grass, a pointing dog will freeze and assume the classic point: tail rigid, nose locked in on the bird. A good pointer will not move from the point position until told to do so by its handler.

Less highly trained dogs, much like my own, will run around a field, hopefully within shotgun range (but not always) until they stumble over a bird or a bird's sent trail. Sometimes, they will point, but usually, they will immediately scare a pheasant into flight.

Most dogs engaged in hunting pheasants enter the state of "birdy" when they get the scent of a rooster pheasant. When dogs get "birdy" they wiggle in strangely different ways. You can watch the hair on their back move in multiple directions, depending on how close they are to wetting their proverbial pants in excitement.

In either case, it's usually more fun watching the dogs than actually pulling the trigger (mostly because of the miss-factor in many of our shooting attempts).

Cooking pheasants can be problematic. Once plucked and drawn, they resemble chickens. However, unlike chickens, pheasants can turn out very dry if you don't cook them with some kind of moisture.

My favorite receipt is to slowly braise the pheasants, seasoned with salt and pepper, in white wine, either in a pot on the stove or in a crock pot. The wine keeps the bird moist as it cooks. After the pheasant has cooked long enough to fall off the bone, I remove the bones and slice the breast into chunks.

Sauté onion and garlic in olive oil, add some oil-packed roasted red peppers, good Greek or Calamata olives, and some kind of roasted sweet green pepper, like a pasilla. Put the boned pheasant, and the wine sauce in was cooked in, in with the vegetables. That's the end of the part that's good for you.

To the otherwise healthy mix of meat and vegetables, I add a half cube of butter and at least a cup of heavy cream.

Serve that over rice, polenta, or pasta, and stand back.

QUAIL

"**S**top flock shooting," I gently advised my son.

"I'm not flock shooting," he quickly responded.

"Yes, you are," I responded a little louder.

"Am not."

"Are too! Which bird were you shooting at?" I demanded to know.

"Those three that were all lined up in the middle of the covey," he advised me.

That, friends, is flock shooting, and quail will make even the most seasoned hunter figure he can (you saw this coming) kill two birds with one shot.

Quail are the ultimate reality-check game. They are flying lessons in humility. They are also about the most popular game bird in America.

Quail are everywhere and, during the quail hunting season, nowhere. They are easy to find and impossible to find.

In California, we have two subspecies of quail, the California quail, known as valley quail, and mountain quail. In Sonoma County, the quail we see are primarily valley quail, but if you go high enough up into the Geysers area, you can find mountain quail. Mountain quail are larger than valley quail and gather in smaller coveys. Quail are related to pheasants and the American version was originally indigenous to the American Southwest.

Valley quail have a crest, or plume, comprised of six feathers, which droop forward on their heads. The male plume is black while the female plume is dark brown.

Quail are true creatures of habit, and once you have determined the range of a given covey, you can pretty much find them somewhere in that area until they are frightened out of it.

Once the females have hatched their twelve or more chicks, the mother and chicks will join other quail in groups of up to twenty or thirty birds that live together until the chicks have matured. Quail can hatch up to three clutches of chicks a year.

During the day, quail forage for seeds and small insects. In the late afternoon, they find a patch of soft earth in which they dig small depressions with their chests and then take a dust bath in their newly constructed dirt tub.

Quail hunting, like pheasant hunting, is a pursuit that, at its core, teams up a hunter with his dog. Unlike pheasants, which hide quietly in covering vegetation, quail pretty much let you know where they are by their calls. Quail calls are described as "Chicago calls," which are social calls between birds, "pips," which are both contact calls and warning calls, and "squills," which are sexual calls made by male quail.

However, just because you might be able to find quail by hearing them, doesn't mean you are about to enjoy grilled quail. While they prefer to escape danger by running underneath cover, quail can get from standing still to rocket-like acceleration in flight faster than any bird I've seen. And when they start to fly, they beat their wings like a humming bird on steroids. The beating of their wings makes a noise that can instantly make a hunter's stomach flip with surprise. The noise also tends to make the hunter a little . . . tense.

Then, in too many cases, the hunter, like my overly excitable son, will attempt to shoot at the middle of the covey figuring that some of the pellets in his shotgun shell will hit several quail. Nope . . . doesn't work that way.

The key to quail hunting is to expect an explosion of quail from every bush in sight and then, when it does actually happen, aim at one, and only one, bird.

The dog has two jobs. One is to flush a covey from cover if they do not want to expose themselves. The second job is to find downed birds. This second responsibility is critical because the cover in which most Sonoma County quail hide is just too thick to get through (unless you don't mind losing much of your epidermal layer and a large quantity of blood). My Labradors seem to thrive on manzanita and chamise scratches especially if they are sniffing the ground and recognize the scent of quail.

On top of being a great reason to stroll around the countryside on a fall afternoon, quail are unbelievably good eating. Again, as I've consistently counseled in these pages, **DO NOT OVERCOOK GAME**! Wild quail have no fat, and it does not take much heat to dry them out and ruin them.

I like to marinate them in olive oil, chopped onions, garlic and peppers, salt, pepper, and lime juice. I usually barbeque them after they've been in the marinade for an hour or two. Some folks wrap them in bacon first and then barbeque them. I'm just kind of lazy, so I don't usually get around to the bacon part. If you cook them until they are just done, no more than five or six minutes, you will have some of the sweetest, juicy delights nature has to offer.

RABBITS

At the risk of offending my good friend, C.D. Grant, it's time to resume the talk about the consumption of little furry things.

My Italian ancestors, and many of the old Italians around Cloverdale, raised rabbits as a regular part of their diet. (They also kept guinea pigs for consumption, but that's another story.)

Around here, we don't eat that many rabbits anymore, but they have been an important source of protein for local residents for ten thousand years.

There are eight species of rabbit native to California. They are basically divided into three groups, jackrabbits, cotton-tail rabbits, and brush rabbits, known affectionately as "brush bunnies."

Jackrabbits are ubiquitous in the vineyards and hills surrounding Cloverdale. Brush rabbits are less common around the Russian River but are prevalent along the coast.

Jackrabbits make a depression in the soil, called a "form," under the cover of brush, and use it to shelter during the day. They are primarily nocturnal foragers, coming out at dusk to feed–and have sex. Jackrabbits can have five or six litters a year, with two or three young in each litter; there's a lot of rabbit canoodling going on most evenings.

Jackrabbits eat herbs and grasses, but will forage on most any kind of greenery, including the bark of fruit trees and your newly planted vegetables. According to the University of California, jackrabbits do not need a regular supply of water. They take their hydration from the plants that they eat.

As their name might indicate, brush rabbits shelter in thick brush. They can also be seen hiding in rock outcroppings. While jackrabbits will travel on regularly used trails between sources of food, brush bunnies rarely stray far from their sleeping areas. Brush bunnies live on grasses, clover, and the woody parts of berry bushes.

Jackrabbits primary defense against predators is speed and evasive actions. Brush bunnies rely on the cover of their habitat to protect them. Because of this, Jackrabbits are more fun to hunt, but brush bunnies are better eating.

Rabbit hunting is one of California's most popular shooting activities. It is a sport particularly suited to families and young hunters. Rabbit hunting is more popular in the Central Valley and the southern desert than Sonoma County. The valley and deserts have wide-open stretches to walk, an abundance of game, and little in the way of people or structures in the way.

Rabbit hunting is done with small arms, ordinarily, small-gauge shotguns or .22-cal. rifles, which are easy for kids to handle and inexpensive to buy.

It's more fun to hunt rabbits with a dog, but rabbit hunting can ruin a dog for upland bird hunting. When you are just about to creep up on a pheasant that you know is holding in a bunch of brush, the last thing you want is for your dog to take off after a rabbit.

But dogs are useful for jackrabbits because, even with a dog on its tail, a jackrabbit will typically turn and head back the way it came. There's nothing more disconcerting than being charged by a jackrabbit being chased by your own dog! Shoot where?

The Native Americans of California, including Baja, used throwing sticks as a primary rabbit hunting weapon. While there were many different shapes to hunting sticks most of them look, remarkably, like the Australian aboriginal boomerang.

Tree branches of one to three inches in diameter were bent using the heat from a fire. Then rocks, or other branches or roots, were used as a fulcrum to bend the branch. The arc of the stick went from a very slight bend to sticks that looked like a shepherd's crooks.

Once the bend was put in the branch, it was shaved on the sides to make it flat like the classic boomerang. The edges were often sharpened or other parts of the stick whittled to add aerodynamics or impact power.

Usually, the stick was thrown in a very flat trajectory, with the concave edge leading. The basic technique was to cripple a rabbit by skipping the stick across the ground and taking out its legs from behind. The hunter would then run up to the disabled rabbit and dispatch it.

The local Pomo used sticks, bows and arrows, slings, snares, traps, dogs, spears, pits, and knives to capture rabbits. While deer hunting was primarily a male-dominated occupation in the Pomo culture, children and women were invited to enjoy rabbit hunting.

Besides the meat, the Pomo treasured rabbit fur for robes and blankets. These they used to get through the long wet winters around here.

The old Italians always told me that it takes more energy for your stomach to digest a jackrabbit than you can get from eating one. That may be true, but if prepared right, jackrabbits are pretty good to eat. Read pressure cooker! Brush bunnies can be fried or braised in broth with wine and herbs.

When cleaning and skinning rabbits, you should always wear plastic or rubber gloves. Rabbits can carry tularemia, an infectious bacteria. Tularemia is nasty stuff that can make you about as sick as you want to be for a month or more. Some cases get into your glandular system and can cause serious damage.

RATTLESNAKE

recognized the shriek that came from across the pool area as having emanated from one of my rugby buddy's wives. With a sinking heart, I realized that she had opened the wrong cooler. It was the one into which I'd thrown the marinating rattlesnake while waiting for the coals to cool in the barbeque.

She and I made up and she even deigned to taste the snake. (Yes, Dad, it tastes like chicken.)

Rattlesnakes are one of those messages from nature that say, "Don't get too comfortable out here." They are one of the elements of nature that keep foraging an interesting proposition.

With warming spring weather, the snakes leave their winter dens where the females have given birth to multiple little stingers and try to get their blood back to operating temperature. Being cold-blooded, the snakes must change location to use sun and shade to regulate their body temperature.

During March and April, you can still find snakes holed up in caves and dens. This is a good time to not put your hand in caves past where you can see the entire interior.

Flat rocks in the sun are favorite warming stations for rattlesnakes through the spring. Come June, when the daytime temperatures start to get up there, rattlers will move out of the sun fairly early and find some shade until the sun starts down again.

Hollow logs and downed timber provide shade for snakes that are close to sources of food and water. There the snakes can work an area but be able to retreat from the midday summer heat.

When you are hiking with your head up, looking for edible things in the woods, always . . . always . . . step up on a log before you step over it. Coming down on a snake, unseen on the other side of a log, will send your undergarments to the laundry.

I've never met a rattlesnake that didn't want to retreat when it had a chance. The only snakes I can say I have routinely seen hold their position were those that were bayed up by a dog or a cat. Given enough time, a snake will uncoil and leave in the opposite direction of a human. I don't, however, usually spend sufficient time around a rattlesnake to tell you that they retreat in every case. Like most woodsmen, I find a way around a snake.

I use to kill every rattlesnake I found. This was pretty much the local ethic shared by woodsmen. I don't go by that rule anymore. I use to eat every snake I killed. Yet, then there's my father again, "Why don't you just eat chicken!"

Over the years, it has become more apparent to me that each of us has an effect on our environment every day. While each little thing we do affects the environment in a small way, the cumulative effect of our acts can change the environment in large ways.

Living amongst the vineyards puts me, and my family, in close contact with rodents of various shapes and sizes. Rodents don't do much for me except eat or destroy anything left in their reach. Snakes eat rodents. It has only taken me thirty or so years of this analysis to determine that if rodents are bad, then snakes are good.

These days, the only rattlesnakes that get killed around our place are the ones that take up lodging in the chicken coop–chickens are good–or those snakes who, after an initial opportunity to remove themselves to the vineyard, are too stupid to take the hint and return to the premises.

Consequently, we do occasionally kill a rattlesnake. A .22 caliber snake shot round to the head is probably the safest way to dispatch a snake. I've never liked shovels much because you have to get too darned close to the beasts to lop off their heads. Sydney Sciaini likes shovels, but she's quicker than am I. She also likes large-gauge shotguns for the job, but that's another story.

The abiding local legend is that if you lop the head off a rattlesnake, you have to bury it. Otherwise, the yellow jackets will eat through to the poison sacks in the head and pass the venom to the next thing, like you, that they bite. It's never been proven that I know of, but . . . *you never know*.

Once the head is off, you can peel the skin back into an inside-out tube, like skinning a salami. If you tie off the end of the tube, fill it with sand and rub it with salt, and then you can hang the skin up to dry. Once it's dry, treat the inside of the skin with glycerin until the whole skin is supple. All you're doing is replacing the water and snake fluids in the skin with a petroleum base liquid. Then you need a friend to build a headband or belt out of the cured skin.

I marinate a skinned snake in white wine, olive oil, garlic, and Italian herbs. After a couple of hours in the marinade, I barbeque the snake. The meat comes off in long, spaghetti-like strings that are very mild and tender (if you haven't overcooked it).

ROCKFISH

n the olden days, say ten years ago, fishing for rockfish (we always called them rock cod, incorrectly) was like Christmas morning. Every time you reeled up your line rigged with multiple hooks, there was an air of childish anticipation at what presents the sea gods would hand you. You were likely to have a big, if not beautiful, fish on each hook. You never knew what would turn up. It seems like there was no end to the harvest of brightly colored gifts from the sea.

As late as ten years ago, catching rockfish off the Sonoma coastline was an afterthought. Going fishing offshore usually meant chasing salmon until you had a limit or until you gave up because the salmon refused to bite. When all else failed, you could always find a reef and load up on rockies or lingcod.

Not anymore.

The same mindset that ran the buffalo and passenger pigeon into virtual extinction (in the case of the pigeon, actual extinction) fishermen have, by many scientific estimates, nearly wiped out rockfish.

It's not that there are no rockfish, there are. It's just that there are substantially fewer of them than there used to be. However, having learned from our history of pushing species to the edge of extinction (see coho salmon and Atlantic cod), modern game managers have learned to err on the side of caution. The protection of fish populations relies on the preservation of a large enough number of sexually mature fish to insure adequate reproduction.

In the ocean, the rockfish populations have been damaged by overfishing. In the last ten years, commercial fishing has become so effective that it alone can eliminate a species. Commercial rock-fishermen drag enormous nets along the bottom of the ocean, using wheels larger than found on a semi tractor-trailer to roll along the bottom. These nets clear-cut the rock reefs where rockfish reside. They take everything in their path and destroy the reef as they roll across it.

Modern electronics, most especially sonar, let fishermen focus directly on the schools of rockfish, ensuring that little time is wasted in scooping up as many fish as possible per drift.

All of the preceding is why rockfish are no longer an afterthought.

There are a couple of reasons why rockfish are an attractive sport fish. One, they are easy to catch. You rarely have days when rockfish won't bite. First, you find underwater rocks (rockfish . . . get it?). Any sonar device will distinguish a rocky bottom from a sandy bottom. A simple weight gets your line to the bottom, where the fish are. You then have the choice of dressing up the two hooks you are now permitted to use in any weird way you think will attract a fish that will eat practically anything. Feathered jigs, chromed jigs, hooks with plastic imitations of nothing ever seen in nature, or a simple piece of fish stuck on the hook will all work.

Once you feel your weight hit the bottom, you have to reel up some to prevent becoming snagged in the rocks. Generally speaking, rock-fishing is expensive. A lot, I mean, *a lot*, of equipment is lost in the rocks, even by experienced fishermen. Moving the lures up and down in the water will attract fish. That's it . . . it doesn't get more complicated.

Historically, rock-fishing has been done in 300 feet of water or so, using two or three pounds of lead weight to get to the bottom and heavy rods and reels that were used more like heavy cranes to winch fish to the surface.

Currently, rock-fishing is restricted to waters less than 180 feet deep. This, again, is intended to limit the harvest and preserve the breeding stock.

Consequently, most rock-fishing, on both commercial sport boats and private boats, is done with relatively light tackle in relatively shallow water. Most rock-fishing off the Sonoma coast is in water thirty to one hundred feet deep. Many fishermen use lightweight bass rods and freshwater bass lures on rockfish just because it's a lot more fun to catch them that way.

The second reason rockfish are so popular is because they taste good. That "red snapper" you see at the fish counter of your store is a rockfish of one variety or another. The meat is white, sweet, and mild. The fillets lend themselves to about any kind of preparation, from frying to baking to grilling. Most, I expect end up as fish and chips, deep-fried in batter.

My favorite recipe is a simple dore. Salt and pepper the fillets and then lightly flour them. Dip the fillets in a thin egg wash, and then fry them in butter until just beginning to brown . . . do not overcook these fish. Take the fillets out of the pan and add a little white wine and lemon juice to the pan. Stir the wine and juice around until all the little cooked bits of flour and things have been scraped off the bottom of the pan and the liquids have begun to simmer. Pour the sauce over the fish and serve.

You can skip the egg wash and do the same thing. Add a little olive oil to the butter to raise the smoke point. This lets you fry the floured fish at a little hotter temperature and the crust will get a little crispier.

SALMON

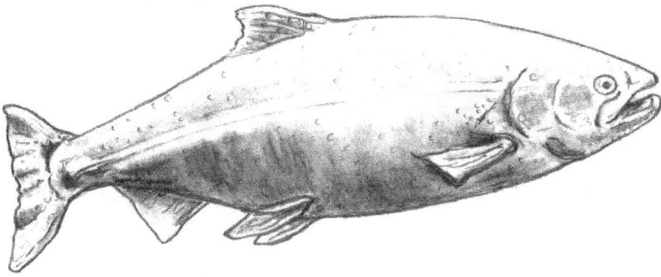

Five miles off the Sonoma coast, the air smells like somebody vacuumed it for every trace of civilization.

It's not hard to look back on our beautiful coastline from that distance and imagine what this country looked like before the arrival of the Europeans. In the cool morning sunlight, the rolling hills rise gracefully out of the sea. In wooded canyons, low-hanging fogs refuse to leave their hollow resting places.

In April, when the ocean salmon season opens, the hills still appear green from offshore. By the time the last king salmon has been boated in September, the hills will be parched brown and windblown.

The opener of the salmon season signals the commencement of the summer offshore fishing season. It's a time to get equipment and fishermen back in tune with the flow of ocean fishing.

Of course, the primary piece of equipment for this endeavor is a boat: usually a largish boat. You don't have to have your own boat, but it's a lot more fun being in control of your hunt.

The commercial "party boats" that work out of Bodega Bay are great fun and provide a pretty sure chance of catching a fish. The skippers are on the ocean every day during the salmon season and have a good idea of where the salmon are to be found on any given day. The price is usually right for the amount of work these guys put into getting fish for their customers.

King salmon are the quarry. In April, most of the fish will weigh ten to fifteen pounds. This year, many larger fish have already been landed. This apparently is a result of the regulatory efforts applied to the catch of "forage fish": anchovies, sardines, and herring. The restrictions on taking forage fish have provided a bumper crop of bait fish and, since these fish are the primary diet of king salmon, there is a bumper crop of salmon.

The ten to fifteen-pound fish patrolling off the coast in April will approach forty pounds in September as they get ready to ascend the rivers of their birth.

Early in the season, the preferred method of angling for salmon is by trolling. An anchovy is inserted into a clip-like device that is attached to an angler's line. A flat piece of brightly chromed metal, a flasher, is attached to the line ahead of the anchovy, and ahead of that, some type of weight is attached. The whole arrangement is dropped over the side of the boat, thirty or so feet of line, "thirty pulls," are stripped off the reel, and the whole mess is pulled behind the boat until a salmon decides to attack it. Frequently, metal or plastic lures, usually resembling something that actually swims in the sea (but sometimes not), are used in place of the anchovy.

The effect of either a baited line or a lure remains the same. For hours upon hours, you either look at your rod, waiting for it to bend over double with the weight of a mad king salmon, or you stare at the lovely Sonoma coast.

In between fish, there is time for sandwiches, beverages, stories, lies, and naps–lots of naps unless you are driving the boat. Sometimes, the sun even shines and, occasionally, it's warm. Usually, you will need to bundle up as the coast usually stays around sixty degrees most of the summer.

One of the best parts of owning an ocean salmon boat is the radio chatter. Men have forever joked about what they perceive to be the inane chatter that goes on between women at sewing bees, whist parties, and in the middle of major league baseball games. Those ladies have nothing on salmon boat skippers who spend long dull days waiting for some fish to make a mistake. The range of gossip, black humor, and general bullshitting is astounding. And seemingly endless.

Usually, however, the radio chatter slows down by noon except for the cryptic comments, that are code between friends, used to describe where they have found fish. God knows, there is no way some guy is going to let anybody, except his buddies, know where he caught one of the million or so salmon off our coast. Somebody else might get all the fish!

After all the preparation and waiting, when you do hook a fish, it is one of the all-time great adrenalin rushes. Salmon are big, strong, and fast. And, owing to the fact that you can use only barbless hooks to catch them, very hard to land. I've seen many hardened men openly pray while fighting a big salmon, and nearly as many reduced to near tears when a big one breaks off.

Then there's always the fun of reeling in the five-pound head of a beautiful king salmon while a sea lion (a.k.a. "furbag") swims off with the other fifteen pounds of fillets–always my favorite moment.

Barbequed fresh wild salmon fillets, crusted with herbs, salt, and pepper is the taste of summer. But to enjoy them in the exhausted languor produced by a day on the ocean, with a cold one in hand, is summer itself.

SMALLMOUTH BASS

Ahh ... spring! And the forager yawns and stretches and goes looking for his foraging stick.

Spring means bass. Not the bass involving eighteen-foot, metal flaked, 200-horsepower speed wagons with trolling motors and sonar that can see through kryptonite and live wells built to jack up the catch for big tournament money, but plain old bass.

My favorite bass fishing is the Russian River smallmouth. Smallmouth fishing in the river is about the least enjoyed, and maybe the most fun, fishing we have around here.

This time of year, the smallmouth do what most other bass do this time of year, building nests and working on the next generation of "bronze sides." From now through the summer, the motivated forager can chase smallmouth from Cloverdale to Jenner.

Most of the smallmouth I've caught run in the one to one-and-a-half-pound range, although I've caught plenty in the two or greater range. The secret is really in movement. You pretty well have to cover miles of river to fill a stringer with your five-fish limit. There is no size limit in the Russian River for smallmouth, but you should probably stick to the twelve-inch rule, as that size is linked to reproductive maturity.

A canoe, your own or one rented from a local outfit, is a good vehicle, although any small pram or float tube will do. The idea is to cover a lot of river.

The bass hang out under the overhanging willows and other riverside foliage, so presentation is a little tricky. It's best to get to solid ground so your casting is true. The bass don't necessarily hold in the same water as steelhead, so you don't need to look for bottom structure like logs or boulders. They tend to hang back in the willow roots and sweeper branches.

My favorite lure is a Rebel crawdad in the smaller sizes. These tend to be easy to present and draw through the structure since their diving lip pulls them under the branches. Use a light or ultralight spinning outfit for the accurate casting required along the river bank. Anything up to eight or ten-pound test-line is fine. Of course, a five-weight fly rod, with a popper or spider pattern, will add a little adventure to your efforts and will hook a lot of fish.

By far, the best bait for smallmouth, as it is for all fish, is live bait. A drifted half-nightcrawler with a large split-shot is killer. The absolute best live bait is a secret that the old timers will tell only with some prodding: eels.

In the springtime, the freshwater eels spawn in the river. The eel fry spend their young lives tucked up under old leaves and muck in back waters at the river's edge. Look in humus collections toward the mouth of feeder creeks, where there is a flow of fresh water but where the sun can warm the detritus. The little eels are the perfect drift bait.

It is likely that while casting for smallmouth you will pick up a "hardmouth," Sacramento squawfish, or two. These are fun to catch but a trash fish that lives on steelhead smolts. We used to have regular hardmouth derbies, which helped keep the population down. It wouldn't be a bad idea for one of the local service clubs to sponsor a derby one of these summers. I've heard, from the "Old Italians" . . . the other old Italians . . . that during the depression, the hardmouth were cleaned, skinned, and cooked in pressure cookers until the bones softened sufficiently to be edible. The fish, meat, bones, and all, were mixed with a binder, breadcrumbs, and egg and made into fish cakes. I've been told they kept a lot of families alive in the early thirties.

Smallmouth fillets are just about the sweetest meat you can pull out of water. You can bread them with anything. Of course, good old corn flour is great, but I even like to use seasoned bread crumbs or cracker meal. Fry them up in butter, olive oil, or bacon fat. They make a great breakfast.

You have to remember that the DFG, in their infinite wisdom, has banned the use of bait and barbed hooks in the river from April 1 through October. This is ostensibly to protect the salmon and steelhead, although I've never seen a steelhead hooked on a chicken liver set out for catfish . . . but more on that later. That means that summer smallmouth fishing is limited to using lures.

While you're out on the river during the early spring, keep your eyes open for watercress and miner's lettuce. Both are excellent this time of year. The watercress looks like tiny bunches of round, flat parsley that only exists in flowing fresh water. The miner's lettuce looks like little frisbees on a stick. It's also not too late to pick dandelion leaves before the plants begin to flower.

No matter what you end up with, a day working your way down the Russian, foraging stick in hand, feels like spring itself.

SEAWEED

S econd thoughts were ricocheting between my ears like a meat-bee over a plate of fried trout. I mean, it wasn't like I hadn't eaten enough sushi to know that seaweed was at least edible, if not downright scrumptious.

But there it was on my plate, fresh from the ocean, staring me down.

If I had some mild concerns, there were nothing compared to the look of dread on my companions' faces.

I'd assembled three plates of seaweed, picked that morning, after a successful abalone dive. Figuring simplicity was the easiest way to get to the heart of the matter, I dressed each plate of raw greenery (or redery or brownery, depending on the variety of weed) with a simple oil and vinegar dressing. The brown one was bitter, the reddish one was bland, and the green one was sweet and delicious if, albeit, slightly rubbery, in a slimy kind of way. (I have the same reaction to lychee fruit, so consider the source.)

One of the plates contained an interesting pink and white arrangement that turned out to have virtually no taste but had a texture akin to eating clam shells.

I figured it was time to do a little research.

Pacific Coast seaweeds are actually algae. Generally, they are classified as green, red, or brown algae. The most popular varieties for eating are laver (nori in Japanese), rockweed, sea lettuce, dulse, kombu (*Laminaria*), and kelp.

Laver, which is widely used in sushi, is a deep purplish-red. Its blades are thin and ruffled with a satiny effect in the water. It is found attached to rocks in the intertidal and upper subtidal zones all along the Sonoma coast. Spring is the best time to harvest most seaweeds but especially laver since, by fall, it will have virtually disappeared from the coast.

I find that it is best to take a bucket and a sharp paring knife out to collect laver. Since you generally have to get a little wet to harvest seaweed, I usually gather it after ab diving or spearfishing while I'm still in a wet suit.

The best and freshest algae is collected during minus tides when you can get out beyond the normal surf zone and find algae that isn't as affected by wave action. Seaweed is pretty easy to harvest since it can't generally outrun, outswim, or bite you. You can, however, get banged up pretty well if you do not walk carefully over or around rocks that are usually underwater. The rocks exposed during a minus tide are as slippery as a politician.

As with many other seaweeds, laver is best used after it has been dried. You can put it in a dehydrator, hang it in the sun, or put it in an oven at the lowest setting possible. Once it's dried laver really sweetens up.

According to Patty Bird, the Pomos, notably her grandmother, fried dried laver with ground game meat. I've put dried laver in salad. Reconstituted, dried laver can be used in sushi, soups, or, I expect, with spam and rice in musubi (see Will Jopson for the details). Laver can also be used in tempura. However you use it, laver adds a sweet earthy flavor to food.

Sea lettuce is bright green and floats around in ruffed sheets. It makes a great salad green if chopped small. You can also dry it and use it in stews, soups, or stir-fries.

Kombu, *Laminaria*, is traditionally dried and used to make soup stock. It reportedly aids in softening beans and speeds their cooking, although I have not used it that way.

Kelp is another story. It is so rubbery as to be almost impossible to chew. The only recipe I could find involved slicing the stalks, soaking them for three days in fresh water, and then pickling them.

You can harvest sea plants most anywhere along the coast where there is a rocky bottom. There are restrictions on harvesting in marine sanctuaries, so you should check with a ranger if you are in a park. You can take an aggregate of ten pounds of sea plants per day. You do not need a fishing license to harvest sea plants.

A great source of information on sea plants is the Mendocino Sea Vegetable Company in Fort Bragg. Their website, http://store. seaweed.net, is a great source of information about seaweed and they have many products for sale.

Believe it or not, the sea plants found off our coast really do taste good and they have fed humans for eons. They are fun to harvest and fun to prepare. Just make sure you eat them in front of some friends to enjoy the full measure of their amazement.

SNIPE

I f you are of an age where you remember watching the *Adventures of Spin and Marty*, the 1955 serial that was a feature of the daily Mickey Mouse Club broadcast, then you will not believe a word of this article. But really, and I'll be a blue-nosed gopher if it isn't true, snipe hunting is the real deal. And you can eat them too! Honest!

Snipe are related to woodcock and are indigenous to the entire United States. They are the size of a quail, albeit a slender quail, and are light-brown colored with cream and dark brown chevrons across their back. Snipe inhabit muddy wetlands. Their bills are long, straight, and slender. They use their bills in a "sewing machine motion" to extract invertebrates from mud or moist earth.

Contrary to the historic myth about snipe hunts, they are not conducted at night with a gunny sack. Traditionally, young people, usually first-timers at summer camp, are filled with snipe stories over a campfire, and then they are led into the woods where they are left with a gunny sack, a flashlight, a noise-maker, and the admonition that if they make a certain noise, the snipe will walk into their sack lemming-like. Of course, once positioned, the youngster is left alone in the woods, at night, to ponder his or her relative significance in the cosmos. The rest of the campers retire to the campfire to savor the plight of the young snipe hunters.

Snipe are, in fact, hunted worldwide. In the United States, they were heavily hunted in the late 1800s, almost to the point of extinction. After the depression, market hunting was prohibited throughout the United States and snipe hunting fell out of favor. It is still a serious pursuit in the United Kingdom and Continental Europe.

In California, snipe hunting is regulated by the Department of Fish and Game under the upland game bird regulations. Snipe can be taken from the third Saturday in October and for the following 107 days. The limit is eight birds per day.

Typically, snipe are hunted like quail, while carrying small-gauge shotguns and walking the edges of sloughs or mudflats. If several hunters can organize to hunt together (questionable, but possible), they can surround a mud-flat and keep a flock of snipe moving around the periphery of the mud. That way everyone can get an occasional shot.

Be sure to bring plenty of ammunition. I mean boxes of number-8 shot. If you have ever tried to hunt doves, and are familiar with their ability to dart and dip at high speed, picture the same flight pattern at twice the speed. Because of that speed and evasive ability, snipe are incredibly hard to hit. The little buzz bombs seem to revel in darting in and out of range in what appears to be a taunting behavior. It works on me as, typically, the more I shoot, and miss, the more frustrated I get.

If you are lucky, and I accent lucky as opposed to being a particularly good shot, you will have snipe for the table. Where you get your snipe makes a difference to the birds' taste. If you can harvest snipe from agricultural wetlands where the invertebrates the birds feed on reside in fresh water, the snipe will taste better. If the snipe come from brackish or tidal areas, you may detect a fishy taste.

The traditional Southern method of preparing snipe is to split the cleaned and plucked birds, drench them in flour, and fry them in butter until browned. Then add some white wine and lemon juice and cook slowly for fifteen minutes, or so. **DO NOT OVERCOOK THE SNIPE**. For the last five minutes, you can add some sliced almonds.

I was looking for another snipe recipe and found the following on a website featuring British game recipes. In this preparation, you stuff the snipe with foie gras and truffles, which are seasoned and moistened with brandy. The stuffed birds are then cooked in butter containing chopped truffles and, finally, served with a Madeira sauce. These people take their snipe very seriously.

SPRING GREENS

S pring is truly the best time of the year for cheap, lazy guys (much like myself).

As the late winter chill passes, and the warm spring rains move through the Alexander Valley, the vineyards and hills become my own "Big Rock Candy Mountains."

For those of you too young to remember Harry McClintock's old song about every hobo's fantasy, let me explain. In the Big Rock Candy Mountains, there are cigarette trees (pretty great if you're broke and need a smoke), lemonade springs, a lake of stew, and hens that lay soft-boiled eggs. In short, it's a land where the food is free for the picking . . . and the picking is easy.

Enter Sonoma spring. For the price of bending over, which, granted, is a little harder each year, a hobo, or Cloverdalian, can dine elegantly.

The most popular of the "easy-pickins" is wild mustard. Our vineyards are overrun with the stuff starting in February. Before those fields of mustard yellow flowers appear, the leaves of the mustard plant are perfect for eating.

Wild mustard leaves are smaller than their commercial cousins found in the grocery store. When fresh and uncooked, the leaves taste bright and peppery. It's pretty easy to pick a shopping bag full of them.

Considering an essential fact of most modern farming techniques, i.e., pesticides, it's probably a better idea to wash the leaves before you consume them. But if you can get into a neighbor's organic vineyard, you can eat the leaves raw as you go along picking.

At home, the mustard makes a great salad base. You can mix it with some of the other wild spring greens or commercial greens. Mustard will always spice up whatever it is mixed with.

Take some of the mustard and sauté it in olive oil, add a scoop of fresh garlic and maybe a shallot, and some salt and pepper. This is just a little slice of "free heaven."

The Italians add wild mustard to stews and the liquid of braised meats. Chopped up, it will add color and flavor to pasta dishes.

A little later in the spring, after the mustard has dropped its flowers, the wild radishes explode in a gaudy display of lavender and pearl-white blossoms. You can use several parts of the wild radish. The leaves are extremely tasty for salads when they are very young and small. By the time the flower has bloomed, the leaves turn rough and bitter.

If you can get the seed pods of the wild radish before they start to swell, you can use them in a salad or stir-fry. Again, like the mustard, the leaves and seed pods of the radish impart a peppery taste to whatever you add them to. My research turned up the fact that wild radish is a powerful antioxidant (whatever the heck that means).

Of course, watercress starts to come alive in the spring. If you are fortunate to have a friend with a good spring, and a little area where the spring water can flow in the open, you are likely to have access to the cream of spring greens.

Watercress makes incredible salads. It goes in stir-fry and on salads in place of lettuce or sprouts. Cook watercress up with some chicken broth, a sauteed onion, some garlic, and sweet roasted peppers. Then season the soup, puree it, and finish it off with a little heavy cream. You will never open a can of store-bought soup again.

Stinging nettles, believe it or not, are fabulous in soups, sautés, or creamed. You usually find nettles when you inadvertently step into a bush and regret the experience. If you are intentionally looking for them, go to the moist shady places in the woods. Don't confuse them with catnip, or a number of other similarly shaped plants–they don't taste good.

Choose only young nettle leaves during the early spring. Use work gloves to pull the leaves off the stalk, or you will be reminded why they are called stinging nettles.

Warning: The lawyers made me say this–*do not eat nettles raw* . . . you will regret it!

Don't boil the nettles because it makes them bitter. A gentle simmer for five to ten minutes will deactivate the stingers. The nettle leaves are a great addition to braised meats or soups. They add color and a very sweet taste.

Dandelion greens, sheep sorrel, and miner's lettuce are all treated in much the same way as mustard and are about as easy to gather. Plus . . . they are free!

SQUIRRELS

I f your favorite childhood cartoon involved the adventures of Rocky the Flying Squirrel and his friend, Bullwinkle the Moose, then you probably don't want to read the rest of this column, because, frankly, it concerns the acquisition and consumption of . . . squirrels.

In fact, squirrels are one of the most popular small game animals in the United States.

Tree squirrels, known as "grey squirrels," are responsible for that hoarse, barking sound that you will occasionally hear coming out of the top of oak, madrone, and nut trees. A mature squirrel will run up to eighteen inches long, including its bushy tail, and weigh up to a couple of pounds. They are grey on the top and white on the belly. When they are startled, grey squirrels will cover their head and body with their full tail, theoretically, to avoid predators from above.

Squirrels are nut and seed eaters, so your chances of finding squirrels depend on your proximity to seed or nut-bearing trees. Squirrels tend to stay in the forest canopy but will often forage on the forest floor. As in the fairy tales, squirrels are hoarders who gather food when it is abundant and store it in caches for later consumption.

Grey squirrels live and give birth in "dreys," which are nests usually built in the top-third of trees made from sticks and leaves and wrapped with grasses. Frequently, they will take over old holes in trees abandoned by nesting birds.

Grey squirrels were a staple food of the Pomo. Men and older boys hunted them with bows and arrows and slings. If you have ever hunted grey squirrels, the incredible level of stalking and marksmanship skill of the Native Americans becomes readily apparent. Nonetheless, hunting grey squirrels is great fun.

Squirrel season runs from September to the end of January.

There are a couple of ways to hunt squirrels. You can "still" hunt them by finding a comfortable spot near a food source, where you can sit, concealed, for an extended period of time without moving. This is a pretty good method for those of us who enjoy a good sit-down, but because squirrels move a lot to forage, and because sitting still enough that a squirrel won't see you is very difficult, still hunting isn't the most effective way to hunt squirrels. Getting a squirrel close enough to shoot while sitting still is very, very difficult if you enjoy breathing or don't mind muscle cramps.

Active stalking is a more efficient method of hunting squirrels, and generally more fun too.

While stalking squirrels, you will be confronted with the squirrel's best means of defense, other than being small and fast. When a squirrel sees you coming, it will instantly go to the opposite side of a tree trunk or branch. Add to that the fact that a squirrel can flatten itself against a branch-like melted wax. As a hunter moves under a branch or around the trunk of a tree, squirrels will move to keep the branch or trunk between themselves and the hunter.

This can get downright hilarious. Picture this forager, and a dog more suited to waterfowl, doing the shimmy-shake around an oak tree, like a deranged maypole dancer, with the Labrador at his heels. All the while, a smarter-than-the-average squirrel slides gracefully around the trunk of the tree until it disappears into thin air. What do you tell the dog but . . . "sorry"?

Squirrel hunting is one of those sports better enjoyed with a partner in a team effort. If one hunter can move a bit ahead and fifty feet to the side of another hunter, the second hunter can usually get a decent shot at squirrels avoiding the lead hunter. Unless your buddy is a real chump, you have to change positions once in a while to let him shoot. While scanning the trees, look for anomalies in the foliage. A lump that is out of place could be a squirrel's head or shoulder. That may be all you ever see of the animal, so be ready to shoot.

Shotguns are the preferred weapon for squirrel hunting. Twenty-gauge or .410-gauge guns in 7.5 to 8-shot are adequate for the job. Some folks use .22-cal. rifles, but these, since you are usually shooting up into a tree, tend to be fairly dangerous considering that a .22 cal. bullet can travel upwards to a mile.

Clean squirrels as quickly as you can to avoid ruining the meat. Field dress the squirrels (remove their organs) and cool them quickly.

There are many recipes for squirrel. They are most easily treated like a rabbit. You may flour the entire squirrel and brown it in butter and oil until medium-rare. Add garlic, onions, greens, and tomatoes. Or, you can brown the squirrel, bake it for an hour, and serve it with pan gravy touched up with a splash of brandy.

STEELHEAD

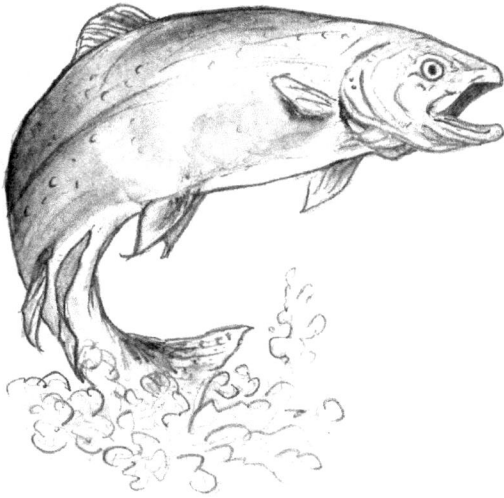

You've got to be loco to chase steelhead. It's a requirement. Take the weather, for instance. Steelheading is only done under overcast skies that emit a steady freezing drizzle. You have to be able to look up into the hills and see pockets of fog holding all day in the hollows.

And it can't just be drizzling, the drizzle has to trickle down the back of your neck–just enough to make you forget the ache in your fingers caused by the constant bath of freezing river water from your line.

Man, is this fun!

Steelhead are a version of rainbow trout that are born in rivers, including the Russian, and migrate to the ocean. Once at sea, they spend three or four years eating fattening up on shrimp and krill and all the other goodies that the oceans have to offer. Studies indicate that they will migrate across the Pacific as far as Siberia and then return to California by way of Alaska. Once off the coast, the fish will find its birth river and return to it to spawn. Unlike salmon, steelhead do not die after spawning, but return to the ocean for multiple years of feeding and spawning.

The steelhead enter the river anywhere from November to April. They follow the river up to the creek in which they were born where they build "redds," which originates from the Old English word "redden" and the Old Norse word "rydhja," meaning "to clear" . . . the things you learn in an outdoor column! Redds are depressions in the gravel, scooped out by the fish, into which they lay eggs and milt.

Cloverdale Creek has an annual return of steelhead as do most of the small feeder creeks into the Russian. My son pointed out baby steelhead in the creek that bisects our property this year. This is after the foot-deep waterway that runs through one hundred yards of buried culvert, which feeds into Oat Valley Creek and then to the Russian. In past years, we've seen adults spawning in our backyards (adult steelhead included!).

Russian River steelhead were planted in New Zealand in the nineteenth century and are the ancestors of that country's rich trout stock.

Most steelhead anglers fish with bait. This is usually a smaller or larger gob of salmon or steelhead roe (eggs). Steelhead travel, and generally stay, at the bottom of the river. To get the bait to them, you have to weigh your line with a length of lead just heavy enough to keep the bait skipping down the river bottom.

Even though I prefer to fish steelhead with flies, bait fishing is a truly tactile experience, one that takes years to master.

When you are in the zone, your fingers and hand feel every little pebble that your sinker strikes through the fishing line. You get to know the difference between a rock, a submerged log, or a gravel bar. When you are in the zone, you don't really look at anything. All your concentration is on the sensations in your hand and fingers that telegraph to you what your bait is doing. Lures can be fished in the same way as bait, letting them bounce down the unseen bottom.

Cast after cast, rock after rock, pebble after pebble, until your line stops and you know it is neither a rock nor a log that has stopped it. Don't ask me how you know—it's just that after X number of years, you just know that a steelhead has stopped your bait or lure with his mouth. That's when you set the hook and hold on.

If it is a wild male steelhead, the first run he takes with your line can be straight up out of the water. I've had steelhead climb stream-side cliffs with their first run. The second run will likely be downstream as the fish tries to let the river help him pull you and your gear into the water. Then it's back upstream and a couple of more head-shaking jumps as he tries to dislodge the hook. The sight of a wild buck steelhead in midair over the river will challenge your bladder control.

I enjoy fly fishing. It's much like bait fishing in that you are drifting an attractant through water in which you figure a steelhead is lying. But the purity of casting a lightweight fly, that I've built at home, to the exact spot I want, seems to make the hours between hits go by more quickly. Additionally, it's way more fun to fight a twelve-pound steelhead on a six-pound test leader with a nine-foot fly rod than on a fifteen-pound test with a seven-foot spinning rod.

In either case, on the Russian, your limit is two hatchery fish per day. You can identify hatchery-raised fish by the lack of an adipose fin on their back just forward of the tail. You cannot keep wild fish. You cannot use barbed hooks to fish during the winter. The regulations are very confusing, arcane, and different from other rivers. Check the regs if you can (a law degree does not necessarily help) before you go fishing.

I don't kill steelhead anymore. There are just too few of them these days. And, in fact, they are just too beautiful, and too grand, to kill. During the summer, those nine-inch trout that are occasionally caught are steelhead. Please release them so they can return to the ocean and grow up.

SURFPERCH

The sun fractured into brilliant golden shards in the surf line just in front of me. The spring sun flashing in my face blinded me momentarily but reminded me that it was, in fact, spring and the surfperch were running.

I don't suppose running is the best description of what surfperch do in the shallows just off the beach in spring. It's more like . . . well, spawning is the polite term.

I keep returning to this theme, but springtime surfperch fishing can really be a great kid thing.

Usually, during March or April, Sonoma County experiences some of the best weather of the year. Breaks in the winter storms can produce cloudless, windless, darned hot days. If your body's thermal settings are not quite ready for summer just yet, a trip to the coast is just the ticket.

Waders are always in good taste as fishing attire in April as the ocean temperature still hovers around the fifty-degree mark even if the air seems summer-like. Still, many people fish for perch in shorts and tennis shoes. It's pretty much up to your tolerance for pain in your lower extremities.

Surfperch fishing is unlike most other ocean fishing. You don't troll for perch nor do you jig for them. Surfperch fishing is much like stream fishing except, rather than dealing with a creek that is generally moving in a single direction, fishing the surf is a multi-dimensional experience.

It's much like a cross between fishing for trout mixed with bass fishing in a washing machine.

Natural baits are the preferred method of take. Here's where the kids can earn their Captain Crunch. The best bait I've found to use on perch are sand crabs. Kids love to catch sand crabs. (But so do I . . . so they have to share!) I grew up on the Bay where catching sand crabs for bait has been elevated to an art form.

Bay shrimp or bits of squid are also good bait and tend to stay on the hook a little longer than sand crabs, but they are nowhere near as much fun to acquire.

In recent years, surfperch fishermen have adopted many of the artificial baits that the bass fishing industry has developed. Plastic Grubs and small plastic worms work pretty well, stay on the hook, and keep your hands clean (thus reducing the actual fun element . . . but women seem to appreciate the thought.)

It's best if you can scout a beach before you go after surfperch. If you can get to the beach at low tide, you can identify the depressions and channels in the sand that are caused by currents. These are where the surfperch hold to feed as waves break above them.

Some folks like a very long rod with a large spinning reel. The long rod helps you keep control of the line and lets you feel the action of the bait. It also lets you feel fish biting your bait and generally lets you cast farther. Shorter bass rods, or spinning rods, are a little more fun once you get a fish on and add a little more sport to the enterprise.

Depending on the surf, you may need a fairly heavy weight to keep your bait on or near the bottom. I've always used tobacco pouches filled with sand. They give you plenty of weight but drift more easily over the sand than do lead pyramid weights. Trouble is, I used to get the pouches I used from my grandfather. I don't believe that Bull Durham is still packaging tobacco like that anymore. Sometimes, you can get the bags at tackle shops.

Cast as far as you can and retrieve the bait slowly toward the beach. This will eventually put your bait in a depression in the sand in which fish are likely to hold. The other option is to use a heavier weight, cast out as far as you can, put your rod in a sand spike (a rod holder used on the beach), crack a cold one, and relax on your beach chair with a good book. As you can imagine, I've employed this method a time or two.

Around here, you can catch barred surfperch, rubber-lip surfperch, red-tail surfperch, and probably five other varieties. Redtails must be ten-and-a-half inches long to keep. The limit is five surfperch.

Surfperch filets are very sweet and fry up nice if you put them in cracker crumbs, corn flour, or bread crumbs (corn flour is my favorite) and fry them quick in peanut oil.

Kids are funny. Once, when my daughter was about five years old, our family spent a couple of weeks at a friend's home on the coast. Each night, Sophie and I would walk down to the cove, I would cast a bait into the rocks, and then settle back with a cocktail. This went on, each night, for most of the two weeks.

Sophie loved our time at the beach. She got to catch the sand crabs and play in the tide pools while I kicked back and watched the sunset.

On our last night, it happened. I caught a beautiful three-pound rubber-lip perch. I was proud that I'd actually caught a fish and called Sophie over to see it. Little did I realize that poor Sophia had no idea why we were spending our evenings on the beach, and the sight of that big iridescent fish flopping on the sand sent her into crying, sobbing hysterics.

The perch was soon returned to the water, and Sophie returned to her mother for consolation.

SURF SMELT

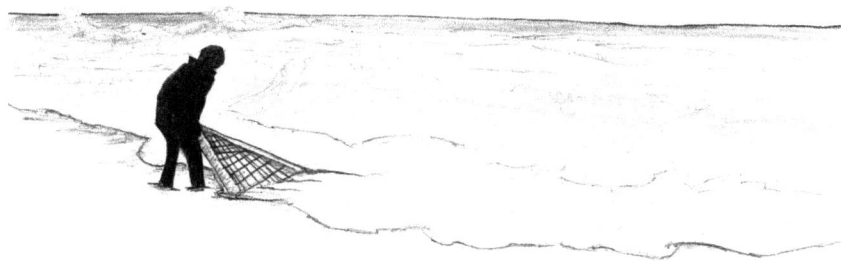

M y wife sat on the beach, in the dark, perched on a five-gallon, white-plastic bucket, muttering to herself and occasionally shouting encouragement. "What the &%#! are you thinking? You're going to be swept away and leave your kids fatherless!"

I remained snug in my neoprene waders as knee-high waves broke in front of me and raced up the beach, through my net, and behind me. I thought of ancient Pomo and Miwok foragers spending nights netting surf smelt, much the same as this, and probably receiving the same kind of spousal support.

Netting surf smelt is one of the forager's most primal endeavors. It is practiced from Sonoma County north through British Columbia.

The basic gear is the "A-frame" net. As far as the internet and I can figure, the original design of the a-frame came to us from the Yurok tribe.

The Yuroks live and fish the lower stretch of the Klamath River near Crescent City. They net salmon as the fish migrate up river, and they have historically foraged the Pacific coast, north and south of the mouth of the Klamath.

The A-frame net is no more than the name implies. Two spars are joined at the end, and a cross brace is affixed about a third of the way down, creating an "A." Netting is attached to the long arms, and to a line that connects the bottom ends of the "A." The netting flows back to form a pyramid-shaped purse. I built the net that I use about twenty years ago. Rather than using wooden dowels for the spars, as are used in most A-frames, I used one-and-a-half-inch box aluminum. While I've watched many of my buddies' nets collapse from rot after not too many years in salt water, my frame looks about the same as when I built it. Periodically, the netting must be changed. You can get the aluminum and other hardware at most hardware stores. The netting is available at many outdoor stores. If you write to me, I'll sketch out a design for you or show you mine (if you show me yours!).

Just to keep it interesting, nature has provided two versions of surf smelt, day fish and, you guessed it, night fish. Surf smelt are found at the high tide, on sandy beaches, from about June through September. They travel in large schools and come up on the beach to spawn. Their eggs and milt are released in shallow water at the top of the wave run. The fertilized eggs work down into the sand and hatch there after a brief gestation period.

Surf fish have modest runs, unlike their cousins in Southern California, the grunion. If you've never seen a grunion run, you should schedule a trip to the sandy beaches south of Los Angeles during the highest July tides. If you're lucky, and at the right beach in the middle of the night, you can see an amazing sight as tens of thousands of silvery grunion glistening in the moonlight stack themselves up a foot deep in a wriggling beach orgy. But, I digress.

Fishing for surf smelt is generally done the same during either the day or night, although fishing them at night is far more unworldly and definitely more exciting. The technique is to stand in the surf line and plant the net into the sand as the waves push the smelt into your net. Some fishermen use Hawaiian cast nets for smelt although that technique is primarily used during the day when you can spot fish in the waves and throw the net to capture those fish.

While I enjoy sunny summer afternoons fishing day fish at Westport, barefoot and in shorts, entering the water off Goat Rock in the middle of a foggy windblown night is pure heaven.

The perfect night fish trip is on a Friday night, in June or July, where there is little or no moon, the light will spook the fish and keep them from coming ashore. Ideally, the high tide will occur shortly after full dark. The south side of Goat Rock at Jenner is my favorite fishing beach. I like to arrive before dark to scope the situation. You look for gulls and pelicans working the water twenty-five to fifty yards offshore. Usually, if the fish are in, you will also see harbor seals and sea lions working in the same area. The key here is if the fish are in. Either they are in or aren't in. It's a question of luck and timing.

Once the sun has gone down, it's time to fish. There is just nothing like prowling a beach at night, up to your thighs in surf, periodically setting your net, and then checking the result. While smelt, fishing I've caught striped bass, wolf eels, and a variety of perch. Sometimes the phosphorescence is stunning. It's always an adventure!

You get to keep twenty-five pounds of fish, although you are not going to want to clean and process twenty-five pounds of fish.

Please, always fish with someone else. I have made the mistake of night fishing alone. Once, while I was the only fisherman on the beach late one Friday night, I was knocked over by a wave, and my waders filled with seawater. I lost my glasses, and almost lost my net, not to mention my life, as I had to crawl back up the beach, on hands and knees, through the surf. It was a long, cold, wet, and blind drive home.

To clean the smelt, get a pair of sharp scissors to clip off their little heads. Then you run your thumb up their stomach to push out their insides. My favorite recipe is a simple tempura one. (Don't forget to chill the batter for an hour!) Deep fry those little puppies, bones and all, until they are crisp as a potato chip on the outside and moist and buttery on the inside. Serve them with salt, pepper, lemon, and some dipping sauce. Surf smelt smoke up perfectly. Brine them in some Kikkoman Teriyaki marinade for a day or so and smoke over alder. They last forever and disappear like candy.

TURKEYS

By the time my butt hit the ground, I guess I'd levitated better than three inches from my resting place against the old fir log. The hair on my neck was still in full panic mode when I turned around to peer over the log at the enormous tom turkey who had gobbled me from ten yards away.

Of course, as soon as I looked at him, my intricate efforts at concealment went into the bag, and the turkey went into the bushes.

Turkey hunting can bring out the absurdity in any hunter's self-image.

Wild turkey hunting is a relatively new phenomenon in Northern California. Turkeys are not native to California, at least not since the white man came west. The earliest recorded turkey sighting in California was in 1877. Since that time, several species of turkey have been introduced in California. The Rio Grande and Merriam subspecies are the most prevalent in the state. Before the 1950s, turkeys were primarily found in the central coast area, below Big Sur.

Since the late 1970s, wild turkeys have migrated throughout the state and began appearing in larger numbers in Sonoma County. Now there are so many that they seem as common as quail.

Adult male turkeys are referred to as "gobblers." Immature males are called "jakes." Hen turkeys are "jennies." Gobblers are easily recognized by their flamboyant head coloration, wattles, and snoods. Gobblers also have "beards." Beards are black hairlike feathers that sprout from a gobbler's chest like a ponytail. Gobblers also have impressively long spurs. You can tell the age of a tom turkey by the length of his spurs. A three-year-old gobbler will have spurs an inch long.

Turkeys' favorite habitat is an oak forest close to a reliable water supply. The oak lands provide roosting areas in the trees and scrub cover on the ground for nesting. Turkeys are delightfully omnivorous. They eat acorns, berries, green plants, insects, and most anything else they can swallow.

Turkey hunting is conducted twice a year. In the spring, from late March to early May, and in the fall during November. In the spring, hunters can kill only bearded turkeys–mature males. In the fall, either sex may be taken. The limit is one bird per day and three per season.

Of all the animals I have the opportunity to hunt, turkeys have to be the hardest to take. Tom turkeys have to be the most alert animal God ever created. With a proper duck call I can talk a wild duck down from a quarter-mile in the sky virtually into my blind. But trying to coax a big tom into the twenty-yard range of my shotgun verges on the impossible.

There are two factors that make turkeys so hard to take. The first problem is that they apparently have X-ray vision.

To hunt turkeys, you need to arrive in the area where you believe turkeys live well before the sun comes up. Then you start listening. Tom turkeys will start gobbling to each other from their roosts about forty-five minutes before the sun comes up. That's when you have to decide where to put your decoys and your blind. Turkey decoys are relatively new. Most are made of very lightweight material, like foam, so that you can carry them easily. Usually, you set out a tom, a jenny, and a jake. The decoys are like a matador's cape to a tom turkey. He wants to run the jake off, kill the other tom, and–you know what he wants to do to the hen.

Toms go crazy at the sight of a well-placed set of decoys. If done properly, the tom will come strutting in, gobbling, with all his feathers stuck straight out, and thrumping his breathing like a bongo drummer.

A turkey hunting blind consists of brush or any other cover that you, in your complete head-to-toe camouflage, can hide in. Having a tree at your back will provide cover and a backrest. You need to be able to see your decoys but must be virtually invisible to any birds coming within a half-mile of your position.

You need to call the toms to get them to look at the decoys. There are a variety of turkey calls available. Most imitate the sound of a hen turkey. You can do this with a diaphragm caller that you keep in your mouth and blow. You can also use a box call that employs a hollow wooden box with a hinged lid that you coat with rosin and scrape against the box to make a hen's chirp. A piece of slate scraped with a wooden rod is an effective hen turkey call imitation.

The problem with this effort is the X-ray vision thing. If you are lucky enough to call a tom close enough that he can see your decoys, he will also be able to see the movement of your carotid artery beating . . . at least that appears to be the acuity of a tom's vision. Then there's the fact that I believe they can hear you breathing from a quarter-mile away. Finally, there's the fact that after sitting motionless for hours, calling turkeys, the slightest effort to relieve muscle cramping will send a tom into the next county.

The second problem is that turkeys are apparently armor-plated. I can't tell you how many turkeys I've shot at, from less than thirty yards, only to see them get hit, fall, then jump up and run away at unheard-of speeds, apparently unmoved by my shot. You must aim for a turkey's head. Their body armor is almost impossible to penetrate.

Additionally, did I say that turkeys can disappear into brush faster than a jack rabbit on steroids?

"So," you say, "use bigger shot." Curiously enough, the American arms industry produces a very heavy shotgun round called a "T." It was designed to hunt turkeys and is just smaller than buck-shot, which used to be used to shoot deer. However, in California, you are restricted to using ammunition no bigger than number 2 shot when hunting turkeys. Number 2 shot was designed to be used on much smaller waterfowl. Get caught hunting with Ts and the fine starts at $750.

The beauty of turkeys, besides the fact that they are just beautiful, is that they are delicious. The Department of Fish and Game has a number of recipes in their very informative pamphlet *Guide to Hunting Wild Turkeys in California*. The pamphlet is on the DFG website, www. dfg.ca.gov/docs/turkeyguide.pdf, and is a great overview of hunting wild turkeys.

However, I would take the recipes in the pamphlet with a grain of salt (in a manner of speaking). Like any wild game, turkeys have almost no marbleized fat. Their breasts are white meat, like a quail, and delicious but will dry out with cooking as quickly as a big tom can disappear into the forest. Moist heat and brining are two ways to keep moisture in the turkey's breast. If you barbeque the breasts, make sure you have a pan of water in the barbeque. Baking the breast in parchment paper after soaking it overnight in a brine of three-quarter cups of salt to one gallon of water is a good way to avoid drying the breast out.

URCHINS

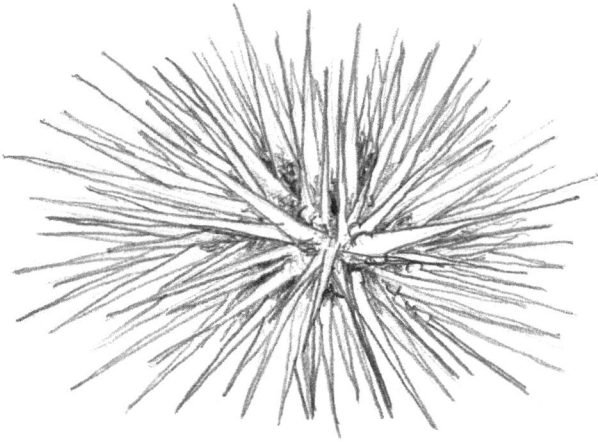

A s I gently juggled the purple pincushion with titanium-reinforced diving gloves, I flashed back to some of the hundreds of urchin spines that have invaded my body–some of which were surgically removed and others that wound up in knees, shins, hands, and forehead, waiting to emerge.

Maybe this was payback–or, maybe it was sushi on the hoof.

I had secured my limit of abalone and dinner was assured. Now, in the abnormally clear water of a Mendocino County cove, I was looking for hors d'oeuvre–sushi uni.

Sea urchins are echinoderms; they are in the same group as sea stars and sea cucumbers. They wear their skeleton on the outside as a shell, which is made up of five fused plates. Pores in the plates hold hinged spines. The spines help the urchin move along the rock floor of the ocean . . . and keep most smart predators off of them (that leaves me out already). The tips of the spines are somewhat poisonous.

The worst thing about an urchin's spines is their nasty habit of breaking off once they've pierced a wetsuit–and the diver's skin underneath. They have backward-facing barbs that keep the broken bits in your body until they fester and pop out–that can take years–or you have them surgically removed.

Urchins eat all kinds of plant material, but around Sonoma and Mendocino, live primarily on algae, kelp, and other seaweeds. Urchins have a mouth centered on their underside, which is ringed with a complex jaw and tooth apparatus known as Aristotle's lantern. They move along the bottom, munching away and having urchin sex. The sex part is pretty tame since eggs and sperm are just ejected into the ocean where, after fertilization, the little offspring swim freely until they begin to develop shells.

Red sea urchins, one of two primary species off our coast–the other being the purple urchins–can keep eating and procreating for up to 200 years.

On the particular day in question, I picked up three large red urchins. As far as I can determine from the Department of Fish and Game's Regulations, you can take thirty-five urchins for private use.

As I was dragging myself out of the surf, my leg happened to become entangled in some nori seaweed. Serendipity . . . all the makings of great table fare.

Back at camp, I started a pot of sticky rice and proceeded to crack the urchins open. Inside the urchin, there is a variety of unidentifiable intestines and runny stuff that I didn't analyze. But there, parked up on each of the five shell segments, were five skeins of roe–urchin eggs. They were colored butter-yellow and had the shape of a flat tongue.

I put the roe sacs on ice and cut the nori into strips while the rice finished cooking. When the rice was cool, I made long balls the size of my thumb and wrapped them in the nori strips, leaving about three-quarters of an inch of headroom. I put the roe sacs on top of the little rice/seaweed columns, set them all up on end like soldiers at attention, and served them to my camp mates with plenty of wasabi and soy sauce.

The sushi disappeared quicker than it took me to pick them up. Unlike the bland uni you typically get at a sushi bar, the fresh roe from the local red urchins has a deep, buttery flavor that is a little slice of heaven when washed down with chilled Sauvignon blanc.

Fresh urchin roe straight out of the shell is a Sonoma coast delicacy you just can't find anywhere else in the country.

WOODRATS

Ever since I started writing this column, I've adhered to the theory that I would eat everything I describe as foragable . . . no matter how strange that material may be.

As I was researching subjects for the column, I came upon an incredible book written by Paul D. Campbell, published first in 1999 by Gibbs Smith, entitled *Survival Skills of Native California*. The book is a thorough review of the tools and methods used by Native Americans in California. One article in the book caught my attention, if not my appetite. So, in an effort to keep the community as educated as possible about the wild food that surrounds it, I present the capture and consumption of the common woodrat.

Please understand that while I have a plentiful source of woodrats in my backyard, I have refrained from eating them because I bait them with poison to keep them out of the chicken coop. The thought of meat marinated in rodenticide does not get my salivary glands going, and I was unable to persuade any of my friends to go on a woodrat hunting expedition in the hills.

Even my Italian ancestors shied away from eating rats. They preferred to eat the guinea pigs that they kept in the chicken coops to fend off the rats, but that's a different story.

The woodrat indigenous to Sonoma County is the dusky-footed woodrat. Woodrats are fourteen to eighteen inches long. Their bodies are gray to brown on top and gray to white on their bellies. They have large round ears and hairy tails that distinguish them from Norway rats.

Woodrats live in stick houses on the ground or in trees. The houses can be up to four feet tall. The houses are also called middens, and one look at one will tell you why woodrats are called pack rats.

They keep and use everything they find to build a home. (My friend Sydney Sciaini is fond of using her flame thrower on woodrat nests. But, again, that's a different story.)

In his book, Mr. Campbell describes the vision of a Native American woman greeting her forager husband gleefully when he arrived home with a half dozen fat woodrats strung in his belt.

The Pomo method of woodrat capture ranged from rousing the little guys out of their stick homes with a specially designed "rat pole" or setting fire to the nest. The idea was to get the rats out of the nest and into the open where they could be dispatched with a stick or a bow and arrow.

The method of preparing the rats for the table is the most interesting part of Mr. Cambell's book. The recipe he reported came from a Kiliwa Indian who hunted rats in the high desert of the Sierra Nevada.

The rat chef would build a small fire and let it reduce itself to coals. He first singed the rats' fur, turning them quickly to avoid burning the little buggers. He then removed the singed hair with a stick. The hairless rats were then returned to the coals and turned once or twice.

After several turns, the rats were removed from the fire and the chef rubbed them with his thumb to clean the skin. He then pulled strips of skin from the shoulders to the tail. These he seasoned with salt from a pouch on his belt. The strips were rolled up and popped into his mouth. These tidbits were said to taste like bacon. Only the rat's tail was removed and not consumed.

The cooked rat's intestines were removed and fed to the dogs. The liver and other soft meats were retained inside the rat. The rats were returned to the coals and were roasted thoroughly.

The chef then set a flat rock next to the fire and found a smaller roundish rock. The rats were taken from the coals and pounded gently between the rocks. This disintegrated the rat's bones and the rat was pounded flat like a tortilla. The rat cake was then folded over and the pounding resumed. When the bones and meat had been bashed completely the resulting pulp was seasoned with salt and consumed with gusto.

Grinding or pulverizing game was a widespread and established Native Californian technique of preserving that game. I encourage anyone to read Mr. Campbell's book. It is very detailed and informative.

Maybe I'll try that rat recipe someday . . . or . . . maybe not. It might taste like chicken . . . or not.

ACKNOWLEDGEMENTS

Thanks to my dad, Frank DeMartini for instilling in me a love of fishing at a very young age, and my mother, Pauline DeMartini for teaching me how to cook. Thanks to the men who taught me about hunting, fishing and camp cooking, Frank and Ray Seghesio, and Bob Sciaini. Thanks also to Cynthia DeMartini for proofreading the manuscript and my son, Gabriel and granddaughter, Nahla DeMartini, for their illustrations.

www.ingramcontent.com/pod-product-compliance
Lightning Source LLC
Chambersburg PA
CBHW071433090426
42737CB00011B/1650